# COUNTER-STRIKE OPERATIONS

DIE WEHRMACHT IM KAMPF

# COUNTER-STRIKE OPERATIONS

## Combat Examples and Leadership Principles of Mobile Defence

F. M. VON SENGER UND ETTERLIN

*Translated by*
LINDEN LYONS

*Series editor:*
MATTHIAS STROHN

**CASEMATE**
*Philadelphia & Oxford*

AN AUSA BOOK
Association of the United States Army
2425 Wilson Boulevard, Arlington, Virginia, 22201, USA

Published in the United States of America and Great Britain in 2021 by
CASEMATE PUBLISHERS
1950 Lawrence Road, Havertown, PA 19083, USA
and
The Old Music Hall, 106–108 Cowley Road, Oxford OX4 1JE, UK

Originally published as Die Wehrmacht im Kampf 22: F. M. von Senger und Etterlin, *Der Gegenschlag: Kampfbeispiele und Führungsgrundsätze der Beweglichen Abwehr* (Neckargemünd: Scharnhorst Buchkameradschaft, 1959)

Hardback Edition: ISBN 978-1-63624-080-0
Digital Edition: ISBN 978-1-63624-081-7

A CIP record for this book is available from the British Library

Printed and bound in the United States by Integrated Books International
Typeset in India by Lapiz Digital Services, Chennai.

For a complete list of Casemate titles, please contact:

CASEMATE PUBLISHERS (US)
Telephone (610) 853-9131
Fax (610) 853-9146
Email: casemate@casematepublishers.com
www.casematepublishers.com

CASEMATE PUBLISHERS (UK)
Telephone (01865) 241249
Email: casemate-uk@casematepublishers.co.uk
www.casematepublishers.co.uk

Front cover: Sniper, Sixth Army, near Stalingrad, September 1942. (Bundesarchiv, Bild 169-0526)

*This book is written in memory of my commander, comrade, and friend,
HANS WILHELM VON HEYDEN, who fell in southern Ukraine
on 22 February 1944 whilst in command of the 26th Panzer Grenadier
Regiment (formerly the 22nd Cavalry Regiment) of the
24th Panzer Division.*

# Contents

# Foreword

The common perception of the Wehrmacht in World War II has been formed by the early years of this conflict, when the German forces stormed across Europe and could only be stopped by the Red Army at the gates of Moscow in the winter of 1941. The concentration on these campaigns has often overshadowed the fact that the Wehrmacht fought defensively for large parts of the war, be it on the Eastern Front as it was trying to stop the 'Soviet steamroller', or on the Western Front. The fascination with offensive warfare is by no means restricted to World War II. Analysing the lessons of World War I, a German officer wrote in 1921 that 'to talk or write about the defensive is a thankless task … only he who thinks, or seems to think, offensively, is thought to be a good soldier'. Battles and campaigns are usually won by imposing one's will on the enemy and by keeping the initiative, which forces the opponent to react rather than act. The defence, in all its forms, is often seen as passive and reactive. However, this view is fundamentally wrong, and in this book, Ferdinand Maria Johann Fridolin von Senger und Etterlin shows the value of the flexible defence at the tactical level, which can break the enemy's offensive power and thus prepare the ground for one's own offensive operations. In German military understanding, offensive action has always formed an integral part of the defence and is characterised by counter-strikes and hasty counter-attacks. The analysis of these lies at the heart of the book.

The book was first published in German in 1959, when the Cold War was in full swing. At the operational and tactical levels, it was always clear that a flexible defence would be necessary should the Cold War ever turn 'hot'. This seemed to be the only chance for the numerically weaker, but technologically superior, NATO troops to stop an invasion by the Warsaw Pact. The book that you, the reader, hold in your hands has to be seen in this context. It is more than a mere historical study; it was intended to provide tangible lessons for NATO in order to prepare the alliance for the next major war. The comments about nuclear warfare in the book show that Senger und Etterlin was aware of the fact that things had changed. Nevertheless, he correctly stated that in the realm of conventional warfare, many of the lessons of World War II were still valid. The study also indirectly shows the value that the new Bundeswehr would bring to NATO. As the strongest European land force, the German Army would have had to bear the brunt of the fighting against the Soviet bloc, and the doctrine of the Bundeswehr in its early years showed very clear links to the experiences of World War II.

The book concentrates on tactical episodes of the war on the Eastern Front, in which the author took part, and it thus combines personal experience with doctrinal analysis. His personal experience had prepared Senger und Etterlin well for such a study. He was born in Tübingen in 1923, into a family with a long-standing military tradition. His father was Fridolin von Senger und Etterlin, who rose to General der Panzertruppe in World War II. The author of this book joined the army in 1940, and he gained most of his combat experience on the Eastern Front. He took part in Operation *Barbarossa*, the German invasion of the Soviet Union in 1941, and, in 1942, he was wounded during the battle of Stalingrad. He saw further action on the Eastern Front, and in August 1944 he was wounded during the second battle of Jassy-Kishinev, losing his right arm. This did not end his military career, though. He was transferred to the Army High Command (OKH) before being captured by American forces at the end of the war. After his release from captivity, he studied law in Göttingen, Zurich, and Oxford (where his father had studied, too) and gained a PhD. When the West German Bundeswehr was founded in 1955, he rejoined the colours and had a very successful second military career. He held a number of staff and command appointments and ended his time in uniform as commander in chief of Allied Forces Central Europe with the rank of full general. In addition to his practical military experience, von Senger und Etterlin was also a very active author. He wrote several books and numerous contributions to military magazines. He died in Ühlingen in 1987.

Prof. Matthias Strohn, M.St., DPhil., FRHistS
Head of Historical Analysis, Centre for Historical Analysis and
Conflict Research, Camberley
Visiting Professor of Military Studies, University of Buckingham

# Introduction

'Mobile defence' is a key term that tends to be understood as the antithesis of 'static defence', especially of the kind practiced by Hitler, and that is frequently regarded as the solution to the question of how a stronger attacker can be repulsed.

'Static defence' normally describes holding on to certain positions. Its proponents refer to examples in which stronger attackers were repelled by firmly held lines. It is up to military-historical research to ascertain whether this holds true. While the fight to hold such a line may be heroic, it seems that the value of so doing has been overestimated as far as obtaining success in operational defence is concerned.

This linear thinking has encroached on the way in which the nature of defensive operations should be viewed. In the natural course of the conduct of defensive operations, the defender initially delays the forward movement of the attacker and then brings him to a halt at a particular point in order to be able to launch a counter-strike that will destroy the enemy.

In short, experience had demonstrated that, in defensive operations, the enemy:

- is delayed upon his approach,
- is brought to a halt on key terrain, and, when he resumes the attack,
- is annihilated.

The forms of combat for these three phases of defensive operations are:

- delaying action,
- positional defence, and
- the counter-strike.

Only the first and third phases are mobile. Their relationship to the static second phase that is positional defence has not yet been clearly conveyed in the available literature.

The primary focus of this book is on the two mobile elements. It will be shown that the mobile forms of defensive operations were used extensively during World War II. Even if it appeared as if lines were held through positional defence, this static phase had in fact always played a subordinate role. Small panzer battle groups were responsible for the conduct of defensive operations, and they developed tactics in this regard which, astonishingly, have thus far found no expression in the official principles of leadership. Perhaps this is because the circumstances brought about by defeat and reconstruction provided little opportunity to learn from and make use of the experiences that had been gained.

This book is intended to help with the clarification of ideas and the establishment of principles that can be developed from an examination of the heavy defensive battles that took place on the Eastern Front.

The author himself participated in all the combat operations that are described as a young officer, troop commander, battalion commander, and regimental adjutant in the panzer troops. He is fully aware that his experiences may lead to conclusions that are not universally valid. Nevertheless, he regards them as sufficiently representative that it seems justifiable to present them to the reader as prime examples of why certain conclusions have been drawn and why certain principles have been recommended.

# CHAPTER I

# Delaying action and delaying formations

## Introduction

Defensive operations against an attack generally begin with the defender delaying the approach of the enemy so that time can be gained to prepare counter-measures. Because of the unusual positional warfare that characterised World War I, the doctrine of delaying action was not properly developed in the interwar period. This is demonstrated by the uncertainty with which the field manual *Truppenführung* dealt with the topic in the years before World War II.[1]

Even during World War II, delaying action was only seldom put into practice. This was because the static positional defence that followed usually led to extended positions that were prone to collapse and that left little room for mobile defence. It was therefore rare for large formations to make systematic use of this form of combat.

Nevertheless, whenever it was necessary for delaying action to be carried out, the art of leadership as practiced by the German Army meant that principles were developed that often ran counter to orders from above and that simply arose in response to the situations that were encountered. Such principles remain applicable today.

Not only small units and formations of company, battalion, or regimental strength but also entire divisions had to employ delaying action

---

1   Heeresdienstvorschrift (HDv) 300/1 – *Truppenführung*, Teil I. The section on delaying action was revised on 1 May 1938 and completely removed at a later date.

by the time our efforts on the Eastern Front began to falter. Ever more were we compelled to conduct withdrawal movements.

It became common after the war to speak of 'delaying battalions', but this creates confusion as to their actual size, so the term 'delaying units' will be used in this book instead. This term is more precise and corresponds better to other terms to be used later: 'positional formations' and 'strike formations'. The following battle case study that deals with southern Ukraine is illustrative of the nature of delaying action. In contrast to the battle case studies that will be examined later, the formation in this example had practically lost all its modern equipment in the whirl of events that accompanied the collapse of the front. The battle fought by this formation played out under conditions that greatly resembled warfare of the kind that may have taken place several hundred years previously. The troops were mainly only armed with rifles and in isolated cases with machine guns. There were no riding horses, and all motor vehicles had long since become stuck in mud. The superiority of the German military and of the German art of leadership therefore had to be proven in a manner characteristic of a past era and devoid of all materiel of the age of technology. Yet the value of the example that follows is that the eternal fundamental principles of combat are to be seen most clearly.

## Battle Case Study: southern Ukraine

### I. General situation

#### 1. Situation in the combat zone of the Sixth and Eighth Armies

In the first few days of March 1944, strong Soviet attack formations broke through the weak German positions along the Ingulets. A particularly deep breakthrough was achieved by the enemy on 6 March to the west of Shirokoye, on the boundary between the German Sixth and Eighth Armies.

The right wing of the Eighth Army lost contact with the left wing of the Sixth Army. Standing along the point of penetration on the right wing of the Eighth Army was the 16th Panzer Grenadier Division and, behind it, the 24th Panzer Division. The forwardmost elements of the panzer grenadier division were completely obliterated, so it was decided that the formation be disbanded and its remaining elements be placed

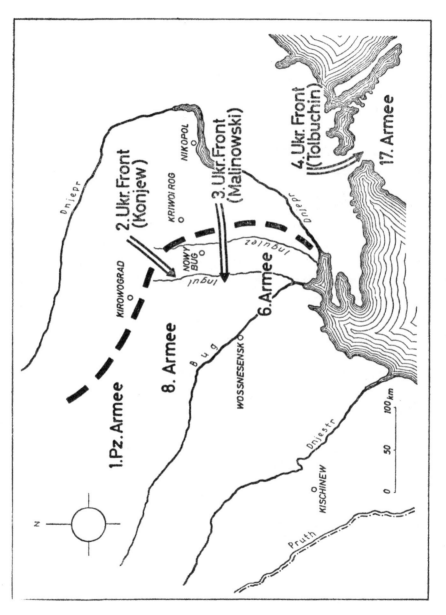

Figure 1: Situation of Army Group South Ukraine at the beginning of the Soviet offensive in the spring of 1944.

under the command of the panzer division. Although the panzer division pushed forward, the position could not be held and, on the evening of 8 March, the bulk of the panzer division fell back to Nikolayevka.

## 2. The enemy situation

The enemy thrust past the southern side of Nikolayevka. Distributed in depth, the Soviet 23rd Tank Corps, the 4th Guards Mechanised Corps, several rifle divisions, and the 4th Guards Cavalry Corps advanced towards Novy Bug. On the northern side of Nikolayevka, the enemy neared Kazanka and drove further to the west. The result was that, on the morning of 9 March, Nikolayevka was threatened with encirclement.

## 3. Weather and terrain

Weeks of heavy rainfall and snowfall had transformed the black soil of Ukraine into mud. There was not a single paved road in the entire area. Only from Novy Bug to Voznesensk was there a partially paved highway. Between the Ingulets and the Southern Bug were a number of smaller rivers that stretched from north to south in the southern part of Ukraine. To the west of Novy Bug flowed the Ingul at the bottom of a deep valley. Another 15 kilometres to the west was a less-deep river valley, the Gromokleya. Yet another 20 kilometres to the west flowed the Gniloi Yelanets River with many tributary valleys.

The terrain of southern Ukraine between the various stretches of river was gently undulating, with elevations of up to 120 metres in some places, often crowned by mounds of earth. Numerous ravines extended like fish bones towards the main rivers, and were generally greater obstacles than the rivers themselves. They were steep-sided and lacking in solid ground at the bottom, and therefore compelled us to make detours of several kilometres.

Natural ground cover was non-existent. The settlements, typically large villages, usually lay hidden in the lowlands near the rivers.

## II. Specific situation

### 1. Situation of the 24th Panzer Division on the morning of 9 March

The forces of the 24th Panzer Division that assembled in Nikolayevka amounted to approximately 6,000 men. Heavy losses had been suffered

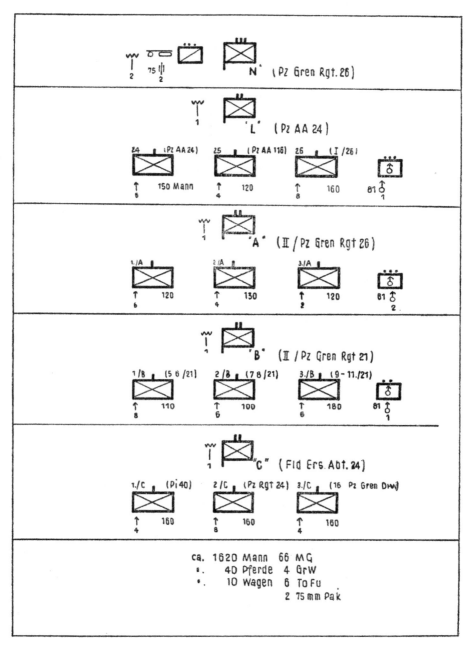

Figure 2: Organisation of Battle Group N on 9 March 1944.

by the panzer division in the fighting on the Ingulets. About 250 motor vehicles of various types were at its disposal, although there was no fuel. Moreover, the troops were exhausted.

The panzer division was reorganised over the course of the following day. Battle Group N was created from all the infantry forces of the panzer division and was to be led by the commander of the 26th Panzer Grenadier Regiment, Colonel Gustav-Adolf von Nostitz-Wallwitz. Immediately and with great energy, the battle group saw to the reorganisation of its fragmented units. Four battalion-sized groups were formed from what remained of the old battalions. These groups comprised mainly their old elements, although they included the scattered troops from the disbanded 16th Panzer Grenadier Division that were condensed into new company-sized units (see figure 2).[2]

It was important to ensure that radio contact could be maintained with the new battalions. The battle group therefore equipped each battalion with at least one portable radio set. The few available wooden wagons were distributed in such a way that each battalion received three or four for the transportation of the radio equipment. In the event of the failure of that equipment, each battalion headquarters would have three or four cavalrymen to be employed as means of communication. Furthermore, each squadron was allocated between two and four horses for the transportation of machine guns and ammunition.

There remained in the zone of Battle Group N a number of armoured personnel carriers of the 24th Panzer Reconnaissance Battalion. As these vehicles could no longer be used for transport and combat due to the mud, it was decided that, once there was success in getting them moving, they would be sent westwards from Nikolayevka to the approximately 250-kilometre distant motor vehicle assembly area near Odessa.

The battle group kept just two medium armoured personnel carriers as towing vehicles for a couple of 7.5cm anti-tank guns, the only means of anti-tank defence available. These vehicles would at the same time be

---

2   The 24th Panzer Division had been formed from the 1st Cavalry Division and, in keeping with its mounted origins, had maintained the golden yellow service colour and terms like 'squadron' and 'cavalry captain'.

used, in addition to horse-drawn wooden wagons, for the transportation of the headquarters staff of the battle group.

It was not long before the disorganised troops had been sorted out and the most important means of transportation and communication that were available had been brought to where they needed to be.

The supply of rations proved to be a considerable challenge. What little food there was to be found in the villages was by no means sufficient. Otherwise, towards the evening, the troops were ready and under the command of a determined leadership. Any commanders unable to assemble any worthwhile forces were either sent westwards or entrusted with other important tasks. For example, a major who could not manage to unite the remains of his battalion was assigned responsibility for a scouting unit.

On the evening of 9 March 1944, the first radio communication exercises took place. Each man was informed of the composition of the new battle group and was told which squadron and battalion he belonged to. For the imminent clash with the enemy, the battle group had 1,620 men under its command. The main weaponry at its disposal amounted to 60 machine guns and four medium mortars. There were no heavy weapons.

## 2. Task of the 24th Panzer Division

The ring of encirclement around Nikolayevka was drawn tighter by the enemy throughout the course of 9 March. That morning, an orderly officer arrived at the headquarters of the 24th Panzer Division and reported that Kazanka, from where he had just come, had been evacuated. He also passed on to us the orders issued by the XXXX Panzer Corps:

1. The enemy is advancing with powerful forces towards Novy Bug.

2. The XXXX Panzer Corps is to delay that advance between the Sagaidak and the Southern Bug long enough so that a new defensive position can be established along the Southern Bug.

3. The 24th Panzer Division, with the remnants of the 16th Panzer Grenadier Division under its command and with its left wing covered by the 15th Infantry Division, will prevent the envelopment of the southern flank of the XXXX Panzer Corps and set up a line of resistance behind the Sagaidak sector.

## III. *Course of the battle*

### *First delaying position*

The troops were exhausted, but the divisional commander knew that there was no time to lose. The front had collapsed completely, and contact had been lost with the formations to the north and south, so the panzer division would have to fend for itself. It would need to prevent the threatened encirclement of its troops and conduct an orderly withdrawal to the first delaying position so as to be able to re-establish contact with its northern and southern neighbours.

After a brief discussion with both regimental commanders and with the commander of the 16th Panzer Grenadier Division, the headquarters of which no longer existed, the commander of the 24th Panzer Division issued the following order:

1. The enemy is presumably near Novy Bug and Kazanka and is pushing further to the west. The forces at his disposal are not known.

2. The panzer division and the elements of other divisions in Nikolayevka will commence a westward withdrawal at 0900 hours. It is the intention of the panzer division to establish a delaying position behind the next ravine.

3. In preparation for this withdrawal, the 24th Panzer Reconnaissance Battalion will launch an attack from 0830 hours against the enemy forces that have already reached the high ground to the west of Nikolayevka with the objective of hurling them back to the north. Any remaining fuel in unarmoured vehicles is to be handed over to the panzer reconnaissance battalion.

   At 0930 hours, the covering forces to the north and south are to disengage and depart for the west. Once this is carried out, the covering forces to the east will also start to fall back to the west. The retreat shall be covered to the north by the 24th Panzer Reconnaissance Battalion and to the south by elements of Battle Group N. Serving as the rearguard will be Battle Group U, under the command of Lieutenant-Colonel Harald Freiherr von Uslar-Gleichen, which has already set up some cover detachments in the east. The first objective to be reached will be the railway line leading to Novy Bug. All immobile vehicles are to be blown up.

The preparations for the breakout took longer than expected. Only by noon were the 20 armoured personnel carriers of the 24th Panzer Reconnaissance Battalion filled up with fuel, mounted, and driven towards the west. Supported by whatever heavy weaponry was still at the disposal of the panzer division, the panzer reconnaissance battalion pushed the enemy back from the high ground west of Nikolayevka towards the north-west. At about the same time, the bulk of the panzer division set off on foot towards the west. All remaining vehicles and heavy weapons had to be blown up. The enemy applied considerable pressure from all sides, and the rearguard units, constantly in combat, were compelled to fall back to the high ground to the west. The enemy pressure abated there somewhat, thereby giving the rearguard units just enough time to gain space to the west. As the battle groups retreated, the enemy forces to their north and south advanced at almost the same pace and almost within visual range.

As the spearheads of the panzer division approached the railway line near Alexandrovka that evening, the enemy security forces on the outskirts of the village withdrew to the west. The divisional commander, who was with the spearhead group, ordered that the entire panzer division move towards the railway embankment on a wide front. The troops stormed forward, in many cases only with cold steel, taking the village and crossing the railway line.

### Second delaying position

During the night, the bulk of the panzer division reached the northern edge of the Sagaidak ravine near Bredikhina Balka. On the morning of 10 March, contact was established in the north with those forces of the 15th Infantry Division that had withdrawn from Kazanka. The panzer division spent the day setting up a position along the ravine and arranging its units behind that position. The right flank of this delaying position was exposed.

Throughout the day of 11 March, the enemy cautiously moved forward against the position with just a few patrol units. Then, on 11 and 12 March, he sent strong forces across the Ingul to the west of Novy Bug. His armoured spearheads thrust along the highway and rapidly reached the Gromokleya. Within visual range of our delaying position, Soviet aircraft landed and unloaded supplies for the enemy columns that were marching through deep mud.

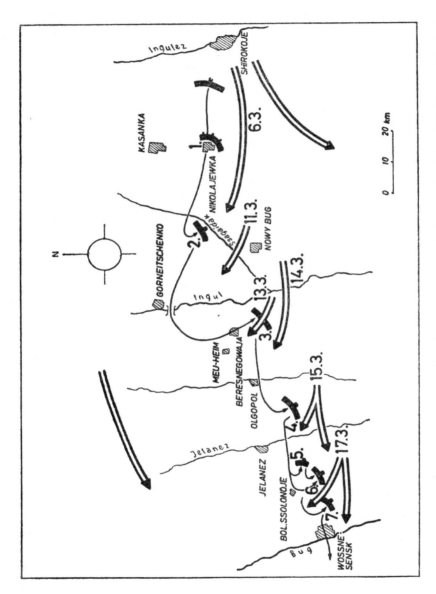

Figure 3: Southern wing of the retreating Eighth Army – Battle Group N (of the 24th Panzer Division) conducted delaying action and thereby hindered the enemy pursuit.

*Third delaying position*

On the evening of 12 March, Battle Group N received the following radio message from the 24th Panzer Division:

> The enemy is advancing along the highway towards Olgopol. The task of the panzer division is to withdraw behind the Ingul and prepare to carry out an attack from the north against the highway. The battle group will disengage tonight and will proceed across the Ingul bridge in Gorneichenko towards the west. It will then radio for further orders.

The commander of the battle group ordered his four battalions to disengage from their current positions overnight and to leave behind only a few covering units. After the battle group had assembled its forces, it set off for the bridge site. It was not pursued by the enemy.

In an exhausting overnight march, the battalions crossed the Ingul north-west of Berezovka and were then given new orders. They were to assemble to the north of the highway in the vicinity of Neu-Heim so that they could then strike the enemy forces on that highway on the morning of 14 March and hurl them back to the south.

On the evening of 13 March and the night of 13/14 March, the battle group moved into the assembly area. Our reconnaissance units pushed forward and discovered that the enemy had already occupied the high ground to the north of the highway and that he had additional forces driving further to the west along that highway. He had also set up multiple gun emplacements.

Two battalions of the battle group launched an attack into a heavy snowstorm on the morning of 14 March, overrunning the enemy positions and reaching the highway in one stroke. The battle group then set up a position from which it would be able to cover the highway with machine-gun fire. As a result, the advance along the highway by the enemy motorised columns was prevented for the time being.

*Fourth delaying position*

On the night of 14/15 March, the battle group was given the order to proceed through Olgopol to the area near Novo-Nikolayevka. The withdrawal of the battle group, constantly in close contact with the enemy, proved to be rather difficult due to the poor state of signal communications. Battalion C, which was committed to the protection of the eastern flank, only received the order to disengage shortly before midnight. In the meantime, Battalions B and L had already departed and were making their way through terrain with no roads whatsoever. The headquarters of the battle group was unable to communicate with its battalions while this withdrawal was being conducted.

The battle group crossed the Gromokleya at the crack of dawn and, after a short rest, moved beyond the eastward-facing covering position of the 257th Infantry Division that lay a little further to the west. Many of the men did not cope with the exertions of this night march through the mud and fell, behind despite the encouragement and often brutal severity of their commander.

On the night of 16/17 March and throughout the day of 17 March, the battle group extended the covering position of the infantry division so that it covered the southern wing between Vozyatskoye and the Gniloi Yelanets River. The enemy attempted to push to the north and envelop the flank of the panzer corps, but his efforts were repelled.

Battalion C had in the meantime caught up with the rest of the battle group. It had served so well as a covering force but was now utterly exhausted. It was in no shape to go into action at that moment, so, in order to give it a head start, it was immediately sent further to the west.

*Fifth delaying position*

Strong enemy forces had continued their unwavering thrust to the west, crossing the Gniloi Yelanets and heading in the direction of Voznesensk. Elements of an enemy rifle division approached Bolshoye Solonoye from the south. The highway led further to the west from there and would be, because of that, of great importance for the subsequent operations of the panzer corps.

The battle group was given the order to retreat across the Gniloi Yelanets on the night of 17/18 March and to push back the enemy forces that were trying to reach Bolshoye Solonoye. Although there was success in finding a point at which to cross the river, it was somewhat vulnerable given that it lay only a few hundred metres behind our cover detachments. Without any clear idea as to what the enemy was up to, the battle group went across the river. The decision to take this risk was made in light of the fact that the troops, who were exhausted and who had not been supplied with fresh rations for several days, could not be expected to make a detour. Commencing with the easternmost battalion, the withdrawal was carried out in echelon formation.

Once on the west bank of the river, the battle group marched through the night by prismatic compass and eventually reached the southern outskirts of Bolshoye Solonoye. Contact was made there with Battalion C, which had already set up a new defensive position. Battalions C and A then departed for the south-east on the morning of 19 March in order to conduct reconnaissance and take up a new delaying position approximately five kilometres to the south-east of Bolshoye Solonoye.

The enemy had already been probing this position throughout the day of 18 March. There had been no German forces to the west of that position up to that point, so it was decided that Battalion L would be committed there so as to prevent any possibility of the panzer division being outflanked. Specifically, the task of the battalion would be to reach Vasilyevka via Hill 117.1 before the enemy arrived there.

The battalion had reached a point immediately to the north of Hill 117.1 in the late afternoon of 18 March when enemy artillery and anti-tank guns rolled into position on the hill with their direction of fire towards the highway. The decision was taken to act at once. One and a half platoons of the battalion seized the hill and took it in one swift motion. Six anti-tank guns and two artillery pieces were captured.

Unfortunately, the spearheads of the Soviet 195th Guards Rifle Division had in the meantime pushed to the north-west and had taken Maloye Solonoye. A small group of German forces, including some of the headquarters staff of the panzer division, had arrived there only a short time beforehand, but it was compelled to fall back to the north immediately. Battalion C was therefore taken out of reserve and sent to establish a westward-facing delaying position against the enemy forces.

On the evening of 18 March, Battalion L advanced from Hill 117.1 towards the south-west, punching through the line of advancing enemy forces and taking Vasilyevka. However, it then had to withdraw to the north during the night.

*Sixth delaying position*

In order to prevent the continuation of the advance of the enemy towards the highway, the battle group was assigned the task of setting up a new delaying position further to the west. It commenced its attack on the morning of 19 March and advanced via Hill 117.1. Battalion A bypassed Vasilyevka, which was occupied by the bulk of the Soviet 353rd Rifle Division, and reached the southern corner of the forest that lay five kilometres to the west of the town. Battalion B attacked the town from the north, but it made little progress until Battalion A struck from the west.

Only in the afternoon did the town fall into our hands. A delaying position was established between the forest and Vasilyevka, and it was from there that the subsequent efforts by the enemy to attack northwards were repelled.

*Seventh delaying position*

Driven off to the south by the attack of the panzer division, the enemy attempted to lunge towards Voznesensk via Ratseva and had, as revealed by our reconnaissance, reached Hills 5.6 and 104.9 (west and south-west of Ratseva) by the morning of 20 March. At 1330 hours, Battle Group N was given the order to disrupt the enemy's progress by taking Hill 112.4. The headquarters staff of the battle group rushed on ahead in four armoured personnel carriers, leaving behind the bulk of the troops of the battle group and hurling the enemy off the hill in close combat. The enemy launched multiple counter-attacks, but the hill remained in German hands. This enabled the 257th Infantry Division to occupy new positions to the south-east of Voznesensk without hindrance. A secure bridgehead was established as planned after that.

The panzer division had successfully put into effect the task assigned to it. That task had been to delay the advance of the enemy between the Ingulets and the Southern Bug long enough for a large bridgehead to be created which would serve as the covering force for the withdrawal of the panzer corps.

## IV. Lessons

The battle case study of southern Ukraine demonstrates that delaying action is possible and can be successful even with completely exhausted troops. The Germans possessed neither tanks nor artillery in the fighting that has been described.

The seven delaying positions were by no means firmly established positions; they were rather imaginary lines traced across the terrain in the orders that were issued that aided the coordination of operations. It was not possible for these lines to be consolidated, given the few forces that were available, although there were occasions where small strongpoints could be set up provided there was enough time to do so. Given that the enemy dictated the rate at which our retreat had to be conducted, the delaying positions could seldom be determined in advance. Even so, we were usually able to evacuate the positions voluntarily rather than in response to enemy pressure, as the Soviets tended to bypass our positions and thrust further to the west.

The distinction made between 'delaying points' and 'strongpoints' in *Truppenführung* is artificial. The only difference in the use of strongpoints in delaying action was that it was the responsibility of the commander, who himself was able to assess the strength of the enemy attack, to determine whether a position should be evacuated (No. 209, Para. 2, Clause 1, TF/G, which is to some degree contrary to Nos 210 and 211). During the withdrawal conducted in southern Ukraine, connecting points could only be sought out and established to the north, for the southern flank of the panzer corps was always more vulnerable. A situation like this is often the case in delaying action.

The seven delaying positions that have been described were the focal points of the delaying action. Four of them (the third, fourth, sixth, and seventh) had to be established by launching an attack. In these four cases, the enemy had succeeded in taking possession of important landmarks or, if not, had come so close to them that it would not have been possible for us to seize them without a fight. However, it was only rarely that natural obstacles could be properly exploited (in this case the second delaying position).

The distance between the delaying positions was on average roughly 20 kilometres. This had more to do with the speed of movement of the enemy and that of our own forces rather than with tactical aspects.

The withdrawal movements from one delaying position to the next were usually carried out at night. This was the case for the movement from the second position to the third, the third to the fourth, the fourth to the fifth, and the sixth to the seventh.

Many of the screening or covering troops who had been left behind to cover the withdrawal movements were lost. This was not the result of combat, for these troops rarely had to fight the enemy, but rather due to their inability to move rapidly through bad weather and across difficult terrain. It ought not to be overlooked that movements could seldom be made in a straight line from one point to the next, as large detours usually had to be made around ravines and through knee-deep mud.

The battle group was always distributed in depth, and the relief of one line of troops by another did not take place. Instead, elements of units that retreated from one covering position were incorporated into the next, with perhaps just a few troops being relieved and dispatched to the third covering position. All the troops that manned the delaying positions, wherever they may have come from, were always placed under the command of the battle group.

Carrying out reconnaissance in front of the first delaying line could only be considered at the outset of the battle. During the course of the battle itself, reconnaissance on the flanks was of greater importance, for it was there that the enemy sought to overtake our troops. Moreover, it was the rate at which he made progress on those flanks that dictated the speed with which our withdrawal had to be conducted.

Envelopment manoeuvres by the enemy could not be prevented from our delaying positions (in contrast to what is stated in No. 200, TF/G). Instead, it was always necessary to execute an attack, a counter-attack, or a counter-thrust to thwart an envelopment. This created time for the establishment of a new delaying line or for the extension of an old one.

# Conclusions

## I. Distinguishing delaying action from other forms of combat

### 1. Conduct of delaying action

In the edition of Heeresdienstvorschrift 300 (*Truppenführung*) from 1 May 1938, No. 45, the 'battle to gain time' was understood to be on an equal par with other main forms of combat. It has often been overlooked that the 'conduct of delaying action' was by no means an element of positional defence. Rather, delaying action was a form of combat that lay between attack and positional defence and made use of elements of both.

It seems doubtful whether delaying action can be conducted in accordance with certain fundamental principles. In other words, even if other forms of combat can be employed for the purpose of gaining time, it is not sufficient to draw upon principles from those other forms of combat when it comes to the conduct of delaying action.

He who wishes to evade a decisive battle does so with the intention of gaining time until a situation arises in which he can determine the outcome of that battle.

If the enemy is seeking a decisive outcome, it is necessary for him to launch an attack. Against such an attack, positional defence might be conducted. However, if the defender is not strong enough to destroy the attacker, then positional defence must give way to delaying action. If, on the other hand, a situation arose in which it was necessary for us, the defender, to seek a decisive outcome, it was usually because there was no more time to be gained. It would have been incorrect in this case to try to delay the enemy further, for example by carrying out attacks with limited objectives. That was why the TF/G rightly classified the 'battle to gain time' as 'delaying action', although it did not clearly distinguish it from positional defence.

The relationship between the following three terms must now be examined: 'attack with a limited objective', 'temporary positional defence', and 'delaying action'. As has been demonstrated by the battle case study of southern Ukraine, delaying action consisted of both the execution of attacks with limited objectives and the establishment of defensive positions for short periods of time. It should be emphasised that an attack with a limited objective is not really any different to any other kind of attack. The same is the case for temporary positional defence in relation to positional defence. The only difference is that the commander who is carrying out delaying action may decide to break off an attack or to abandon a defensive position at any moment he chooses. The generic term 'delaying action' serves to describe this entire process.

The 'attack with a limited objective' and the 'temporary positional defence' can be simply understood as 'attack' and 'positional defence'. After all, attack and positional defence are not unique to delaying action, a form of combat whereby the advance of the enemy is slowed down with the objective of gaining time.

When a commander is given the task of conducting delaying action, it means that he seeks to slow down the enemy by employing a mixture of elements of attack and positional defence. He carries out attacks when necessary and with limited objectives, and he also adopts defensive measures for short periods of time. In this situation, both attack and positional defence serve and are subordinate to the objective of delaying the enemy. Attack and positional defence therefore do not need to be specified when issuing orders to the effect that the enemy must be delayed. However, they absolutely must be specified when some other objective is to be pursued. Should that objective be to hold on to an important piece of terrain, then it is positional defence that should be ordered, but should that objective be to seek a decisive outcome like forcing the enemy back or annihilating him completely, then it is attack that should be ordered.

If, however, the advance of the enemy needs to be slowed down, then the order to be given is to conduct delaying action. It must be left up to the commander responsible for such delaying action to decide how best to carry out his assigned task. He must decide where, when, and for how long an attack is to be conducted or a piece of terrain is to be held.

*2. Withdrawal from action*
Withdrawal from action must be covered by component forces.[3]

---

3   No. 223, Para. 3, TF/G.

The term 'security' is ambiguous and ought not to be used here. It is a word that has been and continues to be frequently misused. If it is used in an order, it is usually because it conceals the uncertainty of the commander who issues that order. Better terms would be 'cover' and 'covering force' or 'screen' and 'screening force'.

It must further be investigated whether 'withdrawal from action' when confronted by an enemy who is applying pressure will always necessarily lead to delaying action. This may indeed be the case if the bulk of the withdrawing forces are to put any distance between themselves and the enemy. However, this question lies outside the scope of this book.

What is certain is that withdrawal from delaying action, like withdrawal from any other kind of action, can only be carried out by leaving behind a covering force. It nevertheless seems doubtful whether a covering force, when pursued by an enemy who is applying considerable pressure, can continue the form of combat that had previously been conducted on the entire front.[4] He who withdraws from a defensive position must assign the covering force the task of delaying the enemy, but he who withdraws from delaying action cannot demand of the covering force that it continue to delay the enemy along the previously existing front in its entirety. Only on smaller sectors can any sort of delaying action continue.

## 3. Mobile operations

Modern armies are fully mechanised, and the distinguishing feature of operations with fully mechanised forces is mobility. Even delaying action is characterised by mobility. It is therefore impossible to make a clear distinction between mobile operations and delaying action. Only occasionally are delaying positions themselves occupied by mechanised troops. The time required to construct fixed positions in modern warfare is too great. Furthermore, fully developed positions are neither necessary nor practical for panzer troops. Even panzer grenadier troops can conduct defensive operations on certain pieces of terrain when on board their vehicles. Armoured personnel carriers can be driven on reverse slopes

---

4    Delaying action can only occur if the enemy is pursuing and applying pressure against a withdrawal. See No. 231, Para. 1, TF/G, whose regulations on delaying action do not otherwise appear to be feasible.

or along perimeter positions and, with their armament, are effective well into the forefield.

Even so, it is necessary for the coordination of operations for lines through the terrain to be identified. Although such lines are perhaps not best described as 'delaying positions', delaying formations should stand along them to face the enemy. It is up to the commander of those formations to determine whether his men establish and occupy fixed positions or whether they mount and go into battle on their vehicles. When lines are mentioned in orders, they serve only to ensure that the delaying formations can work effectively with one another.[5]

As is the case for delaying positions, there is no particular form of combat that is absolutely necessary for 'action between delaying positions'.[6] Until the next delaying line has been reached, the bulk of the delaying formations ought to avoid combat; otherwise, they would be tied down and unable to be reorganised in time. In accordance with the principles of withdrawing from action and conducting a retreat, only the troops left behind as a covering force should fight against the enemy.

## 4. Combat in the cover zone

The tasks of forces that fight in a cover zone, which is placed in front of a defensive position, are the same as those of delaying formations. Attempts have often been made to assign too many tasks to combat outposts. This is usually the result of misjudging what can be achieved from a defensive position and preparing for an attack prematurely.[7]

Since it is the general task of delaying formations to deceive and paralyse enemy reconnaissance, this involves no additional burden as would be the case if they were required to make premature preparations for an attack. Combat outposts are no more than the occupied points

---

5  This can be seen in no. 522 of the field service regulations for the Red Army from December 1943: 'Mobile defence consists of a series of successive defensive actions on predetermined lines of resistance in conjunction with short counter-thrusts that take the enemy by surprise.' It should be noted that mobile defence is identical to delaying action.

6  Nos 212 & 213, TF/G.

7  No. 153, TF/G.

along the final delaying line before the defensive position. They fight unequivocally in accordance with the principles of delaying action.

It seems that 'delaying zone' would be a more appropriate name for the zone that is placed before a defensive position and in which all forces fight in accordance with the principles of delaying action. So that the size of the forces in that zone need not be rigidly fixed, it is sufficient to refer to them as 'delaying formations'.

Combat outposts can be regarded as elements of delaying formations, even if their personnel are drawn from defensive positional formations. Beyond that, delaying formations are the responsibility of the commander in charge of delaying action.

## 5. Cover

The tasks of covering forces overlap considerably with those of delaying formations: providing protection against surprises and gaining time for the bulk of the retreating forces. It must therefore be examined whether covering forces fight in accordance with the principles of delaying action. In the interests of terminological simplification, it seems at the very least to be appropriate to identify 'field outposts along and in front of the covering line' as combat outposts that fight like delaying formations.

He who regards only development, deployment, and reconnaissance as ways to provide cover on the battlefield is lacking in a firm grasp of reality. One of the phrases most frequently seen in orders issued to formations of all types and sizes in mobile warfare was 'formation x is to cover area y'. Nothing else was specified when such a task was assigned other than to conduct delaying action along a certain line against an enemy attack.

## 6. Positional defence

The most important distinction that remains to be made is that between delaying action and positional defence. That distinction can be summarised as follows: while delaying formations are allowed to give way to a stronger enemy, positional formations must hold on to key terrain no matter the strength and composition of that enemy.

The principle of giving way to a stronger enemy has long been understood from the employment of combat outposts and requires only that it be replicated on a larger scale for delaying formations of brigade or divisional strength. Indeed, the principles of combat for smaller units can generally be applied to larger formations. This is because such principles can be put into practice in a variety of situations and are not dependent on the size or organisation of the formation.

It is apparent from this distinction between delaying action and positional defence that the two have different objectives. Delaying formations can delay, but not prevent, the approach of enemy forces of superior strength. However, if those enemy forces are of inferior strength, then their approach can and must be prevented. In such a case, the delaying formations must fight in accordance with the principles of positional defence.

Being prepared for both possibilities is a considerable challenge for a commander who is entrusted with carrying out delaying action. Since the fight against an enemy of inferior strength must be conducted in accordance with the principles of positional defence, all the elements of positional defensive combat are also to be found in delaying action. Those elements must simply be adapted in such a way that the delaying formations are equally capable of delaying an enemy of superior strength.

The placement of delaying positions differs considerably to that of defensive positions. Delaying positions should offer long-range visibility and enable fire to be opened at an early stage, even if it only serves the purpose of disrupting the enemy.

Armoured forces must stand ready along rather than behind the delaying line. Should the enemy forces consist of weakly armoured or unarmoured elements, then the friendly armoured forces can conduct a positional defensive fight against them with their vehicle weaponry. However, should the enemy forces be of greater strength, the friendly armoured forces must delay them for as long as possible whilst also maintaining distance. This applies also for panzer grenadier troops, who should remain mounted on their vehicles so that they can conduct mobile operations, be they counter-strikes or attacks with limited objectives, at the front or on the flanks. Furthermore, by remaining mounted on their vehicles, panzer grenadier troops can withdraw from action and retreat quickly under armoured protection.

As is the case with positional formations, delaying formations form their own combat outposts and reserve forces. These combat outposts fight in accordance with the principles of delaying action on a small scale. Should the enemy successfully cross the delaying lines or seep through between strongpoints, his annihilation must be brought about through the execution of a counter-strike by the reserve troops.

Delaying action at night closely resembles positional defence, as all available forces must be employed to monitor the delaying line. Reserve forces that are held back during the day have to be brought forward to the front at night. It must be accepted that there will be some places along the line where even a weak enemy might concentrate his forces to achieve local superiority, and this means that some ground will have to be yielded. The only way to prevent the enemy from completely overrunning the line is to go over to the defence for a short period of time.

This can be regarded not as a fundamental principle but rather as an exceptional course of action to be employed in a crisis. Even at night, it remains the general principle that only a weak enemy is to be repelled.

### 7. Summary

It is possible for the following conclusions to be drawn:

1. Delaying action consists of elements of attack and positional defence.
2. 'Mobile operations' and 'operations from delaying positions' can be regarded as the same. The 'delaying position' might be more precisely referred to as the 'delaying line'.
3. Cover forces always fight in accordance with the principles of delaying action.
4. The cover zone before a defensive position might more appropriately be called the 'delaying zone'. The combat outposts in this zone also fight in accordance with the principles of delaying action.
5. The main difference between positional defence and delaying action is that the former requires that terrain be held no matter what, while the latter permits ground to be given up to a stronger enemy.

## II. *Principles of delaying action*

### (a) *General principles*

1. Delaying formations are employed to delay the approach of the enemy. They seek to disrupt and immobilise the enemy's ground reconnaissance, to ascertain his intentions and the strength of his forces, and to gain time for the preparation of counter-measures. They are permitted to relinquish terrain and therefore should not allow themselves to suffer heavy casualties or to be tied down by the enemy.

2. Delaying action is carried out by delaying formations along delaying lines. It is up to the commander entrusted with the conduct of delaying action to determine the placement of those delaying lines.

3. Delaying lines are to be held against attacks by enemy reconnaissance units or by other weak enemy forces. As much as possible, the battle should be conducted in accordance with the principles of positional defence and of the counter-strike.

4. Strong enemy forces must be delayed as they approach the delaying line. It is the objective of delaying formations to compel the enemy to make time-consuming preparations for an attack. This is primarily achieved by opening fire at long range, detonating explosives, and setting up obstacles. The bulk of the enemy's forces can be encouraged to fan out prematurely, well before the delaying line, if counter-thrusts are executed against his advance detachments.

5. Delaying formations should withdraw from delaying action at the right time so that they do not get tied down by the enemy. The commander of the delaying formations must decide at precisely which moment such a withdrawal should be carried out. Should a situation unexpectedly arise in which combat at close range takes place with an enemy of superior strength, the commander of the delaying formations can order that the line be held in whole or in part.

6. It is generally a brigade that is entrusted with the conduct of a delaying action. In order to carry out its task, the brigade is assigned its own combat sector.

7.   A division, having assigned one brigade the task of delaying action, can order one or more additional brigades to the same combat sector to provide cover for the delaying formations as they withdraw to a defensive position or a delaying line.

8.   Should there be no such covering force, the commander of the delaying formations must determine for himself the location for a second delaying line and order that it be occupied by some of his own troops so that they can perform the role of a covering force.

*(b) Conduct of battle along a delaying line*

9.   A delaying line is simply an envisaged line that stretches across the terrain. If there are sufficient mobile forces available, it might be possible for the line to be solidified through the creation of strongpoints and fortresses.

10.   A delaying line should be positioned in such a way that it can be held easily by delaying formations against strikes launched by enemy reconnaissance units and weak enemy forces. It should offer good visibility and a wide field of fire that covers approach routes and assembly areas as well as the flanks.

11.   Strongpoints are usually only to be occupied by one or two platoons. Fortresses ought to be positioned so that the entire delaying line, without any gaps, can be monitored. At night, mobile forces or reconnaissance units should be employed to monitor and plug gaps in the delaying line.

12.   Armoured forces should be kept on standby along or behind the delaying line so that they can be used against an attacking enemy. Such an enemy should be annihilated if he is weak or kept at a distance for as long as possible if he is strong.

13.   If an important landmark is taken by enemy reconnaissance forces or advance detachments prior to the arrival of the delaying formations, it is often necessary for an attack with a limited objective to be executed in order to regain control of that landmark.

14.   The moment to withdraw from delaying action must be chosen carefully if it is not possible to do so at night or during periods

of low visibility. In general, the principles of withdrawal from action should be followed.

15. For movement and combat between delaying lines, the principles for conducting a retreat should be followed.

*(c) Coordination of delaying formations*

16. Communications between neighbouring formations are of great importance. It is the responsibility of a superior headquarters to order the locations of connecting points whereby communications can be established and maintained. Commanders of neighbouring delaying formations must have the option of being able to radio one another at any time.

17. A delaying formation without a neighbour on one of its flanks must make some troops available so that it can extend the delaying line to cover that flank. The commander in charge of the conduct of delaying action may decide that neighbouring delaying formations should change places with one another, be that in depth or in width, as they move across the battlefield.

# CHAPTER 2

# Positional defence and positional formations

## Introduction

The second form of combat in defensive operations is positional defence. While terrain can be relinquished in delaying action, it must be held at all costs in positional defence.

In general, positional defence follows a delaying action. A delaying zone often lies in front of a defensive position. Delaying formations fight in the delaying zone, making use of combat outposts at the very least to do so. However, there need not always be delaying zone.

Positional defence always requires the presence of a continuous and fully occupied line. Appearing in place of the main line of resistance is the front perimeter of the defensive position, and it is the responsibility of the commander in charge of this continuous positional system to determine the placement of strongpoints whose purpose it is to stand fast no matter what. Nevertheless, the thoughts and energies of the tacticians are for the most part devoted to the question of how, on a wide front, the areas between strongpoints can be held, even if they are covered by fire from those strongpoints. The answer is that all available forces, including panzer grenadier troops, usually occupy positions near the strongpoints so that they can be employed where needed without delay. Although there is much discussion of the risk of leaving gaps, it is rarely a risk in practice.

This linear thinking has strongly persevered, as it is easier to order that a line be occupied and that the troops wait and see what happens than it is to take a calculated risk and conduct mobile combat. The principles of delaying action and those of the counter-strike are commonly applicable, but both have thus far been regarded as forms of necessary evil and as accoutrements of positional defence that are difficult to put into practice.

Positional defence must be regarded as clearly separate from yet just as important as delaying action and the counter-strike. It must be understood as a form of combat with its own principles of leadership. Delaying action should not be made subordinate to positional defence, and a counter-strike need not necessarily be a consequence of positional defence. All three forms of combat complement one another and are of equal importance.

A proper comprehension of positional defence is therefore one that dissociates it from other forms of combat. At the same time, an understanding of defensive operations ought not to be restricted to positional defence. He who is compelled to conduct defensive operations, be it because the attacker possesses greater strength or because the attacker has temporarily seized the initiative, should not automatically place his forces in immobile positions if they are likely to be subjected to a concentrated attack. This requirement did not arise from the development of tactical atomic weapons, which can be utilised with ease to destroy targets and punch holes in front lines; it is an age-old fundamental principle that was seemingly rendered irrelevant by the abnormal conditions brought about by the weapons and technology of World War I and that was largely forgotten about in World War II.

Positional formations, if conducting positional defence on an over-stretched front, have rarely succeeded in bringing an enemy attack to a standstill or in causing an enemy to bleed to death. It is usually thanks to the highly perfected conduct of battle of armoured strike formations that control can be regained of a 'main line of resistance'. It should be noted that such a main line of resistance is not necessarily of the kind that existed in World War I and that was often specified in orders in World War II, nor is it specifically a front perimeter of a defensive position as conceptualised in *Truppenführung*; it is rather most of the time no more than an imaginary line across the terrain.

The tasks that befit positional formations along or behind this imaginary line and the importance of the role of the mobile strike formations shall be made clear with the aid of the three battle case studies that follow. Since the defensive operations conducted by positional formations can be assumed to be common knowledge, the battle case studies that have been chosen are intended to illustrate the conduct of battle from a defensive position through the lens of the requirements of strike formations.

## Battle Case Study: Nikopol

### I. General situation

*1. Situation and task of Group Schörner (XXXX Panzer Corps)*

From October 1943, Army Group South possessed a strong bridgehead on the east bank of the Dnieper to the east of Nikopol.[8] It was the task of the two army corps committed there to hold on to the bridgehead so as to ensure the safety of the manganese ore mines of Nikopol that were of such great importance to the German armaments economy.

So that the defence of the Nikopol bridgehead could be conducted under a united leadership, it was decided that both army corps would be subordinated to the XXXX Panzer Corps to create Group Schörner. On the right wing of Group Schörner was the XXIX Army Corps with, from right to left, the 335th Infantry Division, the 97th Jäger Division, and the 9th Infantry Division, while on the left wing was the IV Army Corps with, again from right to left, the 17th Infantry Division, the 111th Infantry Division, the 79th Infantry Division, the 258th Infantry Division, the 3rd Mountain Division, and the 302nd Infantry Division.

The infantry divisions of Group Schörner were in bad shape, having lost much of their combat strength and heavy weaponry during the withdrawal battles of the summer of 1943. Their battalions had an average strength of 200 men. All the divisions were committed to the front line, so neither army corps had any reserves at its disposal. The front line was

---

8   Names of locations are in accordance with Military Map L 26, scale 1:100,000, from March 1943.

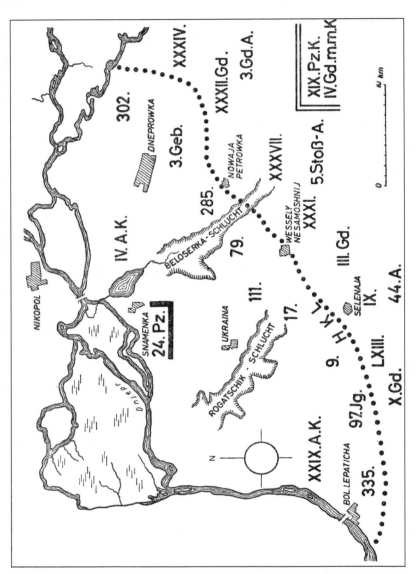

Figure 4: German and Soviet distribution of forces around the Nikopol bridgehead in the middle of November 1943.

weak and made up of only a handful of strongpoints. It was not unusual for each division to have to cover up to 12 kilometres of front line.

Serving as the mobile reserve (the strike formation) of Group Schörner was the 24th Panzer Division. Kept in a central position and ready for action at any time, the forces of the panzer division were organised into multiple battle groups, each of which was led by a regimental commander. The panzer division had been refitted and refreshed and had only just returned to the Eastern Front. Its infantry forces consisted of one light battalion and one medium battalion of armoured personnel carriers, three motorised battalions, and one partially armoured pioneer battalion.[9]

The panzer forces of the panzer division amounted only to a battalion of four squadrons (two assault-gun squadrons and two Panzer IV squadrons), in addition to the headquarters of the panzer regiment. The II Battalion (Panther tanks) of the panzer regiment remained in France near the coast of the English Channel.

Mobility in the conduct of battle would be crucial for the successful defence of the bridgehead, as it would enable the attacker to be struck when he was at his most vulnerable, namely just after he had penetrated the front. It was only at that moment that the superiority of the German leadership in the art of command and in the conduct of mobile operations would be able to be exploited to the maximum extent with the forces that were available. The enemy therefore had to be forced into battle in open terrain.

Nevertheless, any loss of terrain had to be avoided; otherwise, the resulting reduction in size of the bridgehead would make it difficult not only to maintain mobility but also to send in reserves. Furthermore, the enemy would gain a good view of the low ground near the Dnieper and would be close enough to disrupt the flow of traffic over the river bridges.

---

9   The light battalion referred to in the text was the 24th Panzer Reconnaissance Battalion (without the 1st and 2nd Panzer Reconnaissance Squadrons) and the medium battalion was the I Battalion of the 26th Panzer Grenadier Regiment. The three motorised battalions were the I and II Battalions of the 21st Panzer Grenadier Regiment and the II Battalion of the 26th Panzer Grenadier Regiment. Finally, the partially armoured pioneer battalion referred to the 40th Panzer Pioneer Battalion.

Group Schörner considered it to be of great importance that its only reserve, the 24th Panzer Division, be kept on standby so that it could intercept and annihilate any enemy forces that penetrated the front at any time and then follow up with a counter-thrust whose purpose would be to regain control of the old main line of resistance. It was not intended that the panzer division occupy that line. The positional divisions would be put there instead, while the panzer division was to remain behind the line and be ready to move swiftly across the terrain of the bridgehead if necessary.

### 2. Enemy situation (see figure 4)

The Soviet military leadership had assigned the 4th Ukrainian Front the task of eliminating the Nikopol bridgehead and taking possession of the ore mines. Committed along the front of the bridgehead were the 44th Army in the western sector, the 5th Shock Army in the central sector, and the 3rd Guards Army in the eastern sector. Each army comprised between two and four corps, with each of those corps having between two and five rifle divisions. The 4th Ukrainian Front also had a mobile attack force, made up of the 4th Guards Mechanised Corps and the 19th Tank Corps, at its disposal. At the outset of the battle, this attack force amounted to approximately 600 tanks.

Although these Soviet forces had been somewhat weakened over the course of the offensive battles of the preceding few months, they had been continually reinforced with new units from the depths of Soviet territory. The standard of training of rifle formations was quite low, and poorly trained replacements frequently joined the combat troops at the front. It was not unusual for the Soviet military leadership to ruthlessly exploit masses of men in its conduct of operations. The commanders of smaller and medium-sized units and formations were energetic and had become proficient in the art of leadership, although they remained far inferior to the German military leadership in quickly assessing a situation and formulating a decision.

Soviet artillery formations were formidable. Not only had there been a considerable improvement in their performance over the course of the war; there had also been a dramatic increase in their numbers. The rifle divisions of the attack force were fully equipped with artillery, but there also existed entire artillery divisions committed against our strongpoints and equipped with guns of all calibres. The Soviet tank forces were at full strength and topped up with fuel. The tank brigades of the mobile formations possessed the outstanding T-34, the standard model of the Soviet armoured forces and superior to the German tanks present in the Nikopol bridgehead in mobility, firepower, and armoured protection. The rifle divisions were occasionally accompanied by the KV-85 heavy tank, a development of the KV-1 and an immediate precursor to the IS-1. Soviet mobility in the conduct of tank operations suffered to some extent due to a shortage of radio equipment. A tank formation was only equipped with radiotelephones down to the company commander, and it should be borne in mind that a Soviet tank company consisted of 10 vehicles. The result of this shortage was that the tactics put into practice by lower-level tank commanders always followed a systematic and predetermined plan that governed the execution of an attack down to the very last detail.

The motorised rifle brigades of the Soviet mobile formations used trucks only for the transportation of their troops. These trucks came from transport units and were allotted by the high command on a case-by-case basis. When on the battlefield, the motorised rifle brigades had no means of transport whatsoever. Most significantly, they were lacking in armoured personnel carriers. If long distances had to be covered, the rifle troops usually rode on tanks.

*3. Terrain (see map section in the appendix)*

The terrain in the area of the Nikopol bridgehead was a part of the Dnieper River drainage basin. It was the heart of the black soil region of Ukraine, where the rain transformed the ground into mud and made movement impossible for wheeled vehicles and difficult for tracked vehicles.

The bridgehead was divided into three parts by two large ravines that ran from the south-east to the north-west. These were the Rogachik and Belozerka Ravines and would greatly hinder the movement of our reserves, especially in wet weather. Only in Bolshaya Lepatikha and

Nikopol were there military bridges over the Dnieper, and it was across those bridges that the entire supply traffic of both army corps would have to flow.

## II. Course of the battle (see figure 5)

From the end of November 1943 until the middle of January 1944, the 4th Ukrainian Front launched eight large-scale attacks against the bridgehead. What follows is a general overview of how the battle unfolded.

### Attack No. 1

The 4th Ukrainian Front ordered that the first major attack would take place on 20 November. The long-range battle group (the 4th Guards Mechanised Corps) was given the task of breaking through the central sector of the front and penetrating as far as the bridge in Nikopol, while four rifle divisions and several tank brigades would be responsible for expanding the gap in the front created by the breakthrough. After a heavy barrage that lasted three hours, Soviet forces broke through the weak German positions. More than 100 tanks, followed by rifle troops on foot, headed towards Znamenka.

In response to the breakthrough, Battle Group M of the 24th Panzer Division, which had been on standby to the south-west of Znamenka, executed a swift strike against the deep flank of the breakthrough area. The forces employed by the battle group for this strike were a panzer battalion, a panzer grenadier battalion, and a panzer artillery battalion, and they pushed as far as Vesely.[10]

Many of the tanks accompanying the Soviet rifle troops were destroyed. The rifle troops themselves pushed further and were caught in the deadly fire of the German panzer grenadier troops. In this critical situation, some of the tanks of the 4th Guards Mechanised Corps were ordered to turn back so as to help with the expansion of the breakthrough area and to counteract the threat of being cut off.

The rifle forces were stopped in their tracks and largely annihilated by a panzer grenadier battalion and a handful of tanks belonging to

---

10 See below for the battle case study on Vesely.

Battle Group H of the 24th Panzer Division. Over the course of the two days that followed, the repeated attempts by the enemy to assault our positions were repelled.

The first attack had failed. It had been based on the classic plan of achieving a breakthrough in a central sector. However, in contrast to the breakthrough battles conducted by the German military in 1940, that carried out by the Soviet military in this attack in 1943 was met by German mechanised strike formations that were able to intervene at the right place and at the right time. The Soviets lost more than 100 tanks, while on the German side only two tanks were damaged.

*Attack No. 2*

It was now the intention of the 4th Ukrainian Front to shatter the German reserves by carrying out an attack against both wings of the bridgehead.

*Attack No. 2a*

On the western wing, the 19th Tank Corps was assigned the task of following up the seizure of the dominant Hill 81.9 by the rifle troops with a breakthrough whose objective was the bridge in Lepatikha.[11] The Soviet rifle troops took the hill on the evening of 28 November, thereby obtaining a good view of the terrain all the way to the Dnieper. During the night, the 19th Tank Corps moved into its assembly area behind the hill. It had approximately 100 tanks of the newest type at its disposal.

Our Battle Group M also moved into position overnight. Its headquarters was fully aware of the importance of the hill, and it was for this reason that it dispatched its panzer grenadier battalion towards the hill in the early hours of the morning. The men of the battalion mounted their vehicles and advanced through enemy barrage and preparatory fire towards the hill, retaking it moments before the 19th Tank Corps rolled forward. From there, it was possible for the observation troops of the panzer artillery battalion to cover the Soviet rifle forces with fire as they attempted to move forward from their assembly area. The

---

11  See below for the battle case study on Hill 81.9.

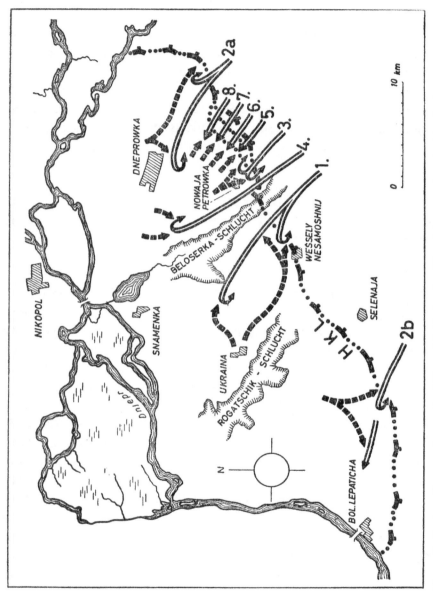

Figure 5: Soviet efforts to destroy the Nikopol bridgehead – The eight major attacks launched by Soviet forces from the end of November 1943 until the middle of January 1944 were countered by the 24th Panzer Division.

panzer artillery battalion and the panzer grenadier battalion managed to separate the Soviet rifle troops from the Soviet tank forces, the result of which was that the riflemen were left behind while the tanks drove in the direction of Lepatikha. The Soviet tanks were hit hard on the flanks by the German tanks of Battle Group M. Only three Soviet tanks made it as far as Lepatikha, but they were destroyed by the garrison force in the town.

### Attack No. 2b

On the eastern wing of the bridgehead, the 4th Guards Mechanised Corps had been fully refuelled and, after penetrating the front, had thrust as far as the area to the south of Dneprovka. Battle Group H succeeded in bringing this enemy to a standstill. The Soviet rifle troops had dug in, so they were struck at night on a wide front by the panzer grenadier battalion of the battle group (the I Battalion of the 26th Panzer Grenadier Regiment). The enemy was taken by surprise and destroyed, enabling the battle group to reach and even move beyond the old front line. With this action by Battle Group H in the east and Battle Group M in the west, the 24th Panzer Division had again been able to thwart the Soviet plan. It had put 70 Soviet tanks out of action without losing any of its own tanks.

### Attack No. 3

After the failure of the first two attacks, the Soviet leadership decided that a different tactic had to be pursued. Any attempt at a deep breakthrough would be abandoned for now in favour of a step-by-step approach designed to bring about the collapse of the bridgehead. Most significantly, two artillery divisions were sent to the front around the bridgehead and were assigned the role of immediately securing any territory that was taken, thereby preventing the success of any counter-strike by German tanks. The new attack commenced on 19 December 1943. After laying down a destructive heavy barrage, the Soviets sent their shock troops, closely supported by numerous tanks, to seize the forwardmost German strongpoints. They did so successfully and quickly set up defensive positions reinforced with full-strength anti-tank batteries. The 24th Panzer

Division had been ready for action, but it did not manage this time to strike the enemy during his advance. Only by carrying out a number of assaults at night could it resolve the situation, but these efforts were costly because the divisional panzer forces could not be utilised to maximum effect. It was therefore the divisional infantry forces that bore the brunt of the fight and that were rapidly worn out. Three German battalion commanders fell on the battlefield in the three days of fighting, yet only 34 Soviet tanks were disabled. Nevertheless, the panzer division managed in the end to retake most of the ground that had been lost.

### Attack No. 4

The 4th Ukrainian Front now believed the German reserves to have been so worn out through the to-and-fro fighting that a central breakthrough with tank forces must finally be capable of success. It was thus that several tank brigades launched a surprise attack on 25 December 1943 and overran the forwardmost German strongpoints. Shortly thereafter, though, they were caught in the concentrated fire of the artillery of the positional divisions and of the 24th Panzer Division.

The unprotected Soviet rifle troops were routed and forced to the ground, but one of the tank brigades pushed further and clashed with a panzer company of the 24th Panzer Division. The panzer company had positioned itself in a depression in the depths of the battlefield and had opened fire at close range. The tank brigade was taken by surprise and, within 10 minutes, 35 of its T-34s were ablaze. The remaining Soviet tanks withdrew after that.

### Attack Nos 5–8

It seemed as if the tactic of trying to achieve a deep breakthrough with tanks would lead to no success whatsoever for the Soviet leadership. It therefore abandoned this approach entirely and ordered that attacks with limited objectives be carried out instead.

On 31 December, the Soviet leadership concentrated its rifle troops in the eastern sector and penetrated the front there. However, before the Soviet anti-tank front could be brought forward, Battle Group H appeared on the battlefield and hurled the attack troops back, in the process of which it disabled 17 T-34s before they even had a chance to roll forward.

The enemy repeated this attack on 12 January 1944, but on this occasion his commitment of materiel was far greater. After an artillery barrage that lasted for several hours, shock troops and anti-tank guns advanced and took possession of the battered German positions. Our counter-attacks by day made no progress against the enemy's defensive fire, while those carried out at night and on foot by the positional infantry and by the panzer grenadier troops of the 24th Panzer Division resulted in heavy losses and only limited success.

On 14 and 17 January, Soviet attack formations penetrated the front in depth. They were supported in their efforts by the gradual and increasingly successful forward movement of the anti-tank front. The German panzer forces were powerless against them, and it was the ever-weaker positional infantry that was burdened with the task of resisting the onslaught. The result was that the bridgehead was slowly being crushed.

After the 24th Panzer Division was withdrawn and sent to another front, the bridgehead collapsed and a significant quantity of materiel was lost. Nevertheless, during the three months in which it had been employed in the bridgehead, the panzer division had destroyed more than 300 enemy tanks whilst suffering relatively few casualties. But this was not enough to stand up to an attacker whose strength was almost 10 times greater than that of our own. Because of this, half of the counter-strikes conducted by the panzer division were doomed to failure.

### III. Lessons

*Counter-strike and counter-attack*

Although the Soviet tank forces had penetrated almost as far as the Dnieper on a number of occasions, they were repeatedly annihilated before being able to consolidate their hold on any territory that had been gained. Their failure was due to the fact that the battle groups of the 24th Panzer Division had fully mastered the tactics of the counter-strike.[12]

---

12  See Chapter 3 for more details on the counter-strike.

Whenever there was success in conducting a counter-strike against the attacking enemy, there was usually also success in rapidly bringing about his destruction. Territory was not lost, and our casualties were few. Success or failure in the conduct of operations by Group Schörner or by the two army corps was dependent on the absolute commitment and freedom of movement of the 24th Panzer Division. Once in action, the battle groups of the panzer division carried out the tasks assigned to them completely independently.

It was often the case that the enemy could not be struck when he was in motion. This was especially so if he had attacked with a limited objective and had immediately, at least partly, gone over to the defensive. It was necessary in such a case for systematic counter-attacks to be launched against the enemy, but the German forces were lacking in strength to do this for an extended period of time. Counter-attacks against a well-prepared enemy were costly, for they depleted the strength of our reserves and by no means guaranteed that the territory that had been lost would be regained. Furthermore, they were unable to eliminate strong enemy forces. The losses of the Soviet defender were presumably less than those of the German counter-attacker.

*Combat with combined arms*

The success of the defensive operations of the strike formations of the German battle groups was generally a result of their ability to make effective use of combined arms. This was only possible through the harmonious organisation of the troops. There always remained a good balance between panzer, panzer grenadier, and panzer artillery troops. A particular advantage for the 24th Panzer Division was that it had two panzer grenadier battalions at its disposal. One of those battalions had been formed from the 24th Panzer Reconnaissance Battalion, and because of this could no longer be expected to carry out reconnaissance activities.

In contrast, the Soviets were lacking in mechanised rifle troops. Their attack forces were therefore unable to work together to the same degree of effectiveness as those of the German military. Without a single unified leadership, the various arms of the Soviet forces often became separated from one another and were thereby eliminated piecemeal.

This was what happened in Attack No. 1. The rifle troops of the Soviet breakthrough group, feeling that they had already achieved a great success, were separated from the tanks that had initially accompanied them. Although this meant that they were in no condition to defend themselves, they pushed onwards. The inevitable result was that they succumbed to the destructive firepower of the German panzer grenadier troops.

In Attack No. 2a, the Soviet rifle troops were separated from the tank forces the moment they left their assembly area. While the tanks continued with the advance, the riflemen were caught in the fire of the panzer artillery troops of Battle Group M. This was the first time during the battle that the panzer artillery troops had gone into action.

Although the Soviet rifle troops managed in Attack No. 2b to exploit the armoured breakthrough and seize territory, they were not ready to defend themselves quickly enough. Consequently, they were taken by surprise and destroyed at night by the numerically inferior panzer grenadier troops.

In Attack No. 4, the concentrated artillery fire of the German forces proved to be sufficient to shatter the Soviet forces that had penetrated the front.

The breakthroughs that had been achieved by the enemy in Attack Nos 1, 2a, and 4 would have seriously threatened the existence of the bridgehead if mechanised rifle troops had been at his disposal. These troops, protected against artillery and infantry fire, would have been able to follow directly behind the tank forces.

## Combat with panzer grenadier troops

If the German forces had made use of unarmoured infantry, they would have been too slow to intervene at the decisive locations to oppose Attack Nos 1 and 2a, and they probably would have been unable to withstand the Soviet barrage fire. In Attack Nos 2b and 3, unarmoured infantry would have been incapable of overcoming the enemy riflemen once they had gone over to the defensive. However, the main reason for our superiority was that the enemy had not yet mastered the tactic of immediately bringing forward his anti-tank guns. Furthermore, he was frequently taken by surprise when attacked at night by armoured personnel carriers. He managed to neutralise this advantage of ours later in the war, for he learnt to fully exploit his anti-tank guns and to properly illuminate an area through which we might be attacking.

Only Attack Nos. 5–8, despite being limited in scope, truly endangered the bridgehead. The mobile German strike formations had no opportunity to hit the attacker during his movements, for those movements were short and quick and remained constantly under the protection of his anti-tank guns. He created what was in effect an anti-tank front, as there existed one heavy anti-tank gun for every 10 metres of front line. The anti-tank front developed into one of the most dangerous tactics employed by Soviet attack forces. This is a remarkable example of a complete transformation in the use of a weapon, for the anti-tank gun had originally been a purely defensive weapon and had become a decisive offensive one. By making use of one anti-tank front after another, Soviet rifle troops could gradually seize territory and hold on to it, while the numerically inferior German infantry troops could do nothing to stop them.

Given that the Soviet rifle forces are completely mechanised these days, moments of weakness of the kind that the German forces exploited can no longer occur. Deep penetration with fully mechanised formations has once more become the most important way of carrying out an attack, which means that anti-tank fronts and their gradual forward movement are likely to be seen less often.

*Atomic weapons*

There is another reason why the anti-tank front is bound to become less important: it requires an enormous concentration of troops that would be extremely vulnerable to the destruction that can be wrought by tactical atomic weapons.

The counter-strike is carried out in an area that lies between the defensive position and the zone further back in which friendly heavy weaponry is located. If a counter-strike is conducted with atomic weapons, this intermediary area—the strike or interception area—must be completely free of friendly troops. The role of the strike formations is to bring the enemy spearhead to a halt and to encircle the enemy so that his movements are restricted to the intermediary area. The strike formations then hit the area with atomic weapons in order to bring about the annihilation of the enemy. It is the responsibility of no one other than the commander of the strike formations to determine the circumstances under which and the moment at which atomic weaponry will be used. The forces with atomic weaponry at their disposal must therefore be placed under his command.

## Battle Case Study: Moldavia

### I. General situation

#### 1. Situation of the Eighth Army in March 1944

A general overview will now be given of another phase of German defensive operations conducted by an army formation. In particular, the decisive role played by a panzer division in those operations will be demonstrated.

After the withdrawal of all German forces from Ukraine in the spring of 1944, the Eighth Army was given the task of setting up a new defensive front that ran diagonally through northern Romania between the Prut River and the Carpathian Mountains. It was also to seal off the highways running from north to south and hold on to the vital bridge over the Prut in Jassy.[13]

After being transported by air out of Ukraine, the 24th Panzer Division, at the end of March, was the first German formation to arrive in the vicinity of Jassy. The panzer division possessed only about a quarter of its original fighting strength in terms of personnel, while approximately 70 per cent of its vehicles had sunk in the mud of Ukraine.

Little by little, more vehicles arrived from workshops in the rear area. There were 20–40 tanks and assault guns, 40 light and 30 medium armoured personnel carriers, and approximately five self-propelled guns.

---

13 Jassy or Iasi. Names of locations are in accordance with the military map of Romania, scale 1:100,000, from June 1940.

This enabled a panzer battalion to be brought to full strength and another two battalions to be equipped with armoured personnel carriers, while another two battalions were motorised in a makeshift fashion.

The remaining formations of the Eighth Army that had survived the collapse of the front in Ukraine slowly arrived in that part of Moldavia which lay between the Carpathians and the Prut. Romanian replacement and security formations, mostly without heavy weaponry, that stood in the vicinity of Jassy were employed for the construction of the so-called Strunga Defence Line, which ran diagonally through Moldavia.

The construction of this new defensive position took place whilst German forces were in constant combat with the enemy. It was the intention of the enemy to put a stop to this construction and to envelop the left wing of Army Group South Ukraine between the Carpathians and the Prut.

### 2. Enemy situation

The Soviet attack forces were utterly exhausted after the heavy fighting in Ukraine. Their supply had come to a temporary halt, for their routes of supply were muddy and overextended. Only gradually did strong Soviet forces move forward. Nothing stood between the enemy and the Carpathians, as Moldavia and northern Bessarabia were at that stage unoccupied by German troops. Had the enemy wheeled the spearheads of his attack to the south, he would have been able to enter and take a significant portion of Romanian territory. However, the initial objective set by his leadership was to cross the northern stretch of the Prut and to seize Jassy with its railway and road bridges.

### 3. Terrain (see map section in the appendix)

The terrain between the Carpathians and the Prut is dominated by the valley that runs from east to west between Jassy and Targu Frumos. To the south of this valley was an area of forested high ground on whose forwardmost side the Strunga Defence Line was being prepared.[14] There

---

14  Referred to as the Trajan Line in Hans Friessner, *Verratene Schlachten: Die Tragödie der deutschen Wehrmacht in Rumänien und Ungarn* (Hamburg: Holsten-Verlag, 1956), 61 & 66.

were only a handful of routes that cut through this forested area from north to south. The most important of those were the road connecting Husi and Jassy and that connecting Roman and Targu Frumos. Rising to the north of the line connecting Targu Frumos and Jassy was sparsely overgrown high ground composed of thick clay soil. This high ground dropped away sharply in the area north of Jassy to where the Jijia flows.

## II. Course of the battle (see figure 6)

The following outline of the course of the battle is based on an excerpt from a war diary that describes the dramatic duel with the Soviet 16th Tank Corps, which with its overwhelmingly superior strength strove incessantly for an operational breakthrough or envelopment.

### Attack No. 1 (1 April 1944)

Strong enemy rifle forces crossed the stretch of the Jijia that lay to the north of Jassy and created bridgeheads near Rediu Mitropoliei and Epureni.[15] Hurricane-force snowstorms prevented any kind of motorised movement. The 24th Panzer Division assumed command of the Romanian security units stationed in Jassy.

On 2 April, both regiments of the panzer division advanced on foot and struck the enemy, putting a stop to his efforts to expand the bridgeheads.

### Attack No. 2 (5 April 1944)

Enemy forces departed Stanca and advanced through snowstorms, bypassing Vulturu to its east and reaching a point six kilometres from the outskirts of Jassy. The 26th Panzer Grenadier Regiment, assigned the task of thrusting eastwards from Vulturu, committed its I Battalion, on foot, to its northern flank whilst sending its II Battalion, partly mounted on armoured personnel carriers, directly to the east. The troops of the 26th Panzer Grenadier Regiment reached the Prut, thereby cutting off the enemy and enabling the 21st Panzer Grenadier Regiment to annihilate that enemy.

---

15  Refer to the military map of Eastern Europe, scale 1:250,000, NL 35–2, reproduced in the appendix for the locations where this battle took place.

*Attack No. 3 (7 April 1944)*

Romanian infantry forces hastily withdrew when the enemy launched an attack to the north of Vulturu with the 46th Tank Regiment and the 254th Rifle Division. The 26th Panzer Grenadier Regiment, equipped with three tanks that had just been delivered, executed a counter-thrust and destroyed six enemy tanks in close combat.

*Attack No. 4 (9 April 1944)*

The enemy shifted the direction of his attack further to the west, sending several rifle divisions over the road connecting Targu Frumos and Jassy in an advance towards the south. The 26th Panzer Grenadier Regiment remained in Vulturu while the 21st Panzer Grenadier Regiment, with 12 tanks, was dispatched to the west. After Letcani was retaken in an envelopment attack on foot, the enemy forces that had broken through were destroyed piecemeal. The result was the capture of 10 guns.

*Attack No. 5 (12 April 1944)*

The 24th Panzer Division set up a defensive front on the high ground that lay to the north of the road connecting Jassy and Targu Frumos. This front, covered by four battalions, was approximately 20 kilometres in width and extended from the area west of Vulturu to that north of Podu Iloaiei. On standby in Damian was an armoured battle group of 15 tanks and 30 armoured personnel carriers.

The enemy attempted to penetrate this front in the evening in the vicinity of Podu Iloaiei. The formations he employed, belonging to the 16th Tank Corps, were the 109th Tank Brigade, the 15th Motorised Rifle Brigade, and the 78th and 93rd Rifle Divisions. By concentrating all the firepower of our infantry forces, the enemy riflemen were separated from the enemy tank forces, which continued to roll forward through the front line. The armoured battle group then moved against the flank of the breakthrough area and succeeded in disabling all the enemy tanks. The battalion of armoured personnel carriers advanced beyond our front line against the enemy rifle troops that had been left behind by the enemy tanks, and the result was that the enemy riflemen suffered heavy losses and were compelled to retreat.

We suffered no casualties whatsoever!

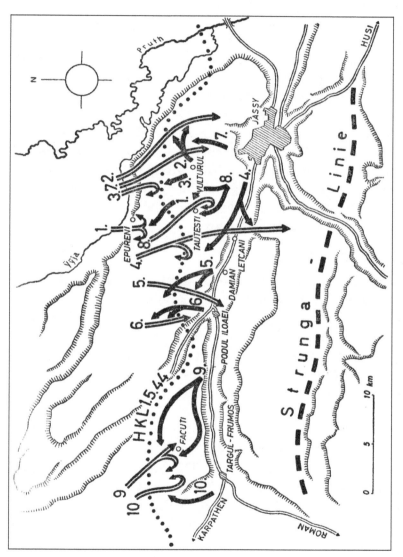

Figure 6: Battle for Moldavia – The Soviet attempts in April and May 1944 to seize the road connecting Targu Frumos and Jassy and to break through to the area between the Carpathians and the Southern Bug were prevented by the intervention of the 24th Panzer Division.

*Attack No. 6 (13 April 1944)*

More German infantry forces arrived slowly and gradually took over responsibility for the positions that had been established. The 24th Panzer Division formed two armoured battle groups, one in Damian and the other in Podu Iloaiei, and each was equipped with 10 tanks and a battalion of armoured personnel carriers. It was to the north of Podu Iloaiei that the enemy penetrated the front with the 50th and 51st Tank Brigades as well as with the 93rd Rifle Division.

The enemy managed to move forward a number of anti-tank guns and to set them up on high ground. Our tanks and self-propelled guns launched a counter-attack against this enemy, and another battalion did the same on foot. In the meantime, the battle group in Damian struck the enemy on his flank. The two battle groups then worked in conjunction with one another to obliterate the enemy guns and to compel whatever was left of the enemy forces to withdraw.

*Attack No. 7 (27 April 1944)*

In the morning, the enemy broke through the front in almost the same location as he did on 5 April and reached a point immediately to the north of Jassy. The entire 24th Panzer Division committed itself to an attack on the enemy flank. All available tanks were utilised, while the remaining troops advanced on foot. Once the enemy forces were eliminated on 28 April, the German troops moved forward to the old line on the high ground that overlooked the Prut.

*Attack No. 8 (29 April 1944)*

The enemy penetrated the front to the north-west of Jassy with the 103rd Tank Brigade and the 207th Rifle Division and approached the Romanian positions near Tautesti. The 21st Panzer Grenadier Regiment was sent by the 24th Panzer Division to the village, and it succeeded, in fierce fighting, in hurling back the eastern flank of the enemy forces that had broken through. Our tanks and armoured personnel carriers then pivoted to the south and annihilated the bulk of the remaining enemy forces from the rear.

*Attack No. 9 (2 May 1944)*

The enemy shifted the focal point of his attack far to the west and thereby succeeded, to the north of Targu Frumos, in achieving a deep penetration of the front with the 16th Tank Corps and two rifle divisions. The 24th Panzer Division then sprang into action. All its panzer units struck the deep flank of the enemy forces, while the panzer grenadier troops carried out a frontal assault against the advancing enemy rifle troops. These riflemen had no tanks accompanying them, for those tanks had been left behind in difficult terrain in the vicinity of Facuti. It was there that the enemy IS tanks were hit from behind and destroyed by our armoured battle group. After that, the entire panzer division launched a concentrated attack and retook the positions on the high ground to the north of Targu Frumos.[16]

*Attack No. 10 (7 May 1944)*

The enemy again achieved a breakthrough to the north of Targu Frumos. Although he resisted tenaciously against a counter-attack conducted by the XVII Army Corps, his forces were eliminated and the positions on the high ground were retaken.

### III. Lessons

*Outcome of the defensive battle*

Over the course of the fighting, the 24th Panzer Division destroyed more than 100 enemy tanks. As a result, the striking power of the enemy breakthrough formations, especially that of the 16th Tanks Corps, was reduced dramatically. Without the almost non-stop intervention of the panzer division, any one of the penetrations achieved by the enemy would probably have led him to tremendous operational success. The German defensive front was consolidated to such an extent during those five weeks that it was possible for steps to be taken to carry out an offensive operation whose objective was to push the front forward to the Jijia. However, the

---

16  See below for the battle case study on Facuti.

panzer forces soon had to be withdrawn from this sector and sent to Poland. The front in Moldavia collapsed shortly thereafter and Romania was lost.[17]

*Conduct of battle*

A close analysis of these 10 actions by the 24th Panzer Division reveals that one was carried out on foot (against Attack No. 1), one on foot and with armoured personnel carriers (No. 2), four on foot supported by tanks (Nos 3, 4, 7, and 10), one with tanks and armoured personnel carriers (No. 5), and three with tanks and armoured personnel carriers and on foot (Nos 6, 8, and 9).

The most successful action was that conducted against Attack No. 5. Without suffering any casualties, our forces destroyed all the enemy tanks that had broken through and repelled the enemy rifle troops. Almost as successful were the actions against Attack Nos 8 and 9.

In all three of these actions (Nos 5, 8, and 9), the main reason for success was the commitment of armoured battle groups composed of panzer troops and panzer grenadier troops under a united leadership. Moreover, these battle groups worked in close cooperation with unarmoured infantry and artillery units.

*Forms of combat*

In this battle, the counter-strike proved to be far more successful than the counter-attack. This is of great significance for the investigation carried out in this book. The actions carried out against Attack Nos 5, 8, and 9 were pure counter-strikes. The difference between the counter-strike and the counter-attack will be explained in detail in the next chapter.

*Key terrain*

If an enemy can seize and set up a defensive position on key terrain, the success of friendly defensive operations is open to question. It becomes necessary to launch an attack against such a position if there is to be any chance of eliminating it.

---

17 This is similar to what happened with the Nikopol bridgehead. See the chapter 'Abtransport der Panzer- und mot. Divisionen' in Friessner, *Verratene Schlachten*, 48ff.

Of great importance for the Eighth Army during the fighting in Moldavia was to hold on to the high ground that lay to the north of the road connecting Targu Frumos and Jassy. At the very least, control of the road itself had to be maintained, and German forces managed to do so throughout the course of the defensive battle. For the XVII Army Corps, it was necessary to prevent the enemy from occupying the hills that overlooked the valley and that would allow him to exert his influence against the road. The enemy attack forces always managed to achieve some initial success, sometimes even taking possession of major strongpoints or key terrain. However, the earlier our strike formations could intercept the attacker, ideally while he was still moving, the greater the triumph that could result from our defensive operations.

## Positional units

There were almost no positional units available at the outset of the battle in Moldavia. No defensive position had been established to ensure that the key terrain could be held. Elements of the 24th Panzer Division often had to be employed to set up defensive positions. Once a cohesive front had been formed, the positional units were too weak to be able to bring enemy attacks to a standstill or to annihilate the forces that were carrying out those attacks.

## The issuing of orders and the chain of command

Due to the ever-changing situation in the non-stop defensive operations that have been described, it was not possible for the 24th Panzer Division to issue detailed orders to the forces, mostly armoured battle groups, at its disposal. It was also not usual for local commanders to be subordinated to those battle groups. Instead, the battle groups were allocated to threatened sectors of the front and instructed to work in conjunction with the positional units. In addition, the battle groups remained largely independent and were given freedom of action. The task they were assigned was general in nature, namely to ensure, on any particular sector of the front, that the main line of resistance or that a certain piece of key terrain be held.

Artillery units or locally formed reserve forces were occasionally subordinated to the battle groups so that counter-strikes or counter-attacks could be conducted under a united leadership. Once appropriate coun-ter-measures had been carried out, artillery and reserve units were handed over to the infantry so that the battle groups could regain full mobility.

## Battle Case Study: Hill 81.9

*I. General situation in the combat zone of the 97th Jäger Division on 27 November 1943*

The 97th Jäger Division had been involved in heavy defensive fighting since 24 November 1943.[18] The enemy had been employing powerful rifle and tank forces to try to hurl back the bulk of the jäger division into the hollow near Schäferei in the hope that this would provide him with favourable jump-off positions for a breakthrough at the bridge site in Bolshaya Lepatikha. The 97th Jäger Division and the XXIX Army Corps had nevertheless managed for the most part to bring the enemy attacks to a halt. The penetration of the front by the enemy had achieved a depth of two kilometres, the result of which was that a wide salient had been formed in the front of the jäger division. Any further penetration of the front by the enemy would bring him dangerously close to the bridge site and supply centre on the Dnieper.

The right wing of the 97th Jäger Division had not yet been attacked, and the dominant Hill 81.9 still remained in the hands of German forces. However, those forces were severely weakened. If the hill were to be lost, movements in our rear area would no longer be concealed from the enemy. In addition, it would have become possible for the enemy to enter the ravine in the sector of the 335th Infantry Division, which, in view of his masterful infiltration tactics in difficult terrain, might have led to the collapse of the entire right wing of the XXIX Army Corps.

Although the enemy penetration in the central part of the sector of the 97th Jäger Division had been neutralised, a shortage of forces meant that it had not been possible to establish a cohesive defensive position. The activity of the enemy shock troops lasted well into the night of

---

18 For an understanding of the overall situation, see the battle case study above on Nikopol.

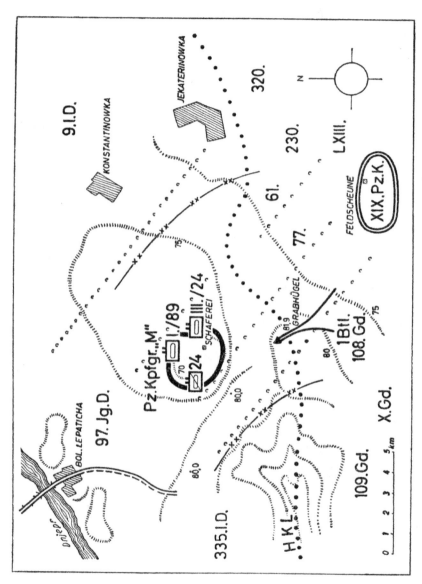

Figure 7: First phase of the battle for Hill 81.9 – Battle Group M of the 24th Panzer Division concentrated its forces in the combat sector of the 97th Jäger Division near Schäferei. On the night of 27/28 November 1943, enemy rifle troops seized Hill 81.9.

24 November, shifting perceptibly to the right half of the sector of the jäger division.

Shortly before nightfall, our aerial reconnaissance reported a strong concentration of enemy forces two kilometres to the south-east of Feldscheune. Amongst them were a large number of tanks. In response to this situation, the XXIX Army Corps requested that it be allocated some forces from the 24th Panzer Division. Accordingly, the panzer division received an order on 25 November to the effect that it immediately dispatch an armoured battle group to the army corps. Battle Group M therefore arrived in the vicinity of Konstantinovka on the night of 25/26 November and assembled in the vicinity of Schäferei on 27 November.[19]

The headquarters of Battle Group M was organised as follows:

(a) Headquarters of Battle Group M (staff of the 24th Panzer Regiment)
   • one pioneer company of armoured personnel carriers (3rd Company of the 40th Panzer Pioneer Battalion)
   • one heavy flak battery of 8.8cm guns (1st Battery of the 287th Army Flak Battalion)
(b) Panzer battalion (elements of the III Battalion of the 24th Panzer Regiment)
   • two assault-gun companies (9th Battery of the 24th Panzer Regiment and the 2nd Battery of the 278th Assault-Gun Battalion), each equipped with 10 StuG III assault guns (self-propelled 7.5cm L/48 cannons)
   • one panzer company (10th Company of the 24th Panzer Regiment) with 10 Panzer IV tanks
(c) Panzer grenadier battalion (24th Panzer Reconnaissance Battalion)
   • two panzer grenadier companies of light armoured personnel carriers
   • one heavy company with:
      o a gun platoon of five 7.5cm L/24 cannons mounted on medium armoured personnel carriers

---

19  The commander of Battle Group M was Lieutenant-Colonel Burkhart Mueller-Hillebrand. See figure 8 for the organisation of the battle group.

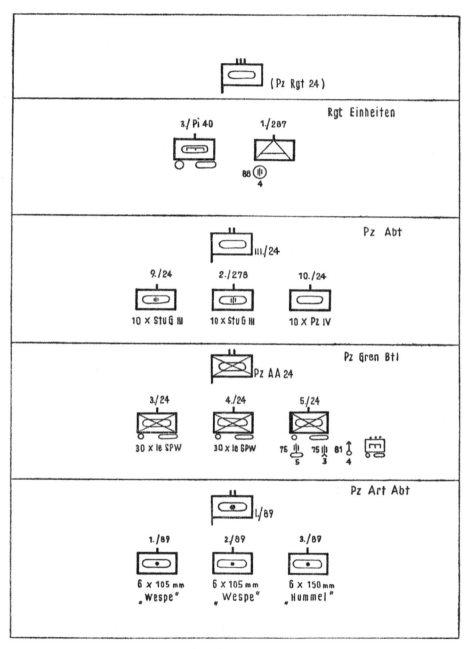

Figure 8: Organisation of Battle Group M on 28 November 1943.

       o an anti-tank platoon of three 7.5cm L/48 anti-tank guns drawn by medium armoured personnel carriers

       o a mortar platoon of four 8.1cm mortars on medium armoured personnel carriers

       o a pioneer platoon of medium armoured personnel carriers

(d) Panzer artillery battalion (I Battalion of the 89th Panzer Artillery Regiment)

- two batteries of 10.5cm Wespe self-propelled howitzers
- one battery of 15cm Hummel self-propelled howitzers

The 24th Panzer Division had been refreshed and refitted in the summer of 1943 and had therefore entered combat near Nikopol at full strength. Even so, the fierce defensive fighting that had been taking place since the beginning of November had taken its toll on the troops. The panzer division had lost approximately a quarter of its vehicles and personnel. Particularly strenuous were the constant movements into positions of readiness, the lack of fixed positions that would have afforded some protection from the open air of the cold nights, and the arduous marches behind the front line of the bridgehead from one crisis spot to the next. Nonetheless, the fighting spirit of the troops had not diminished.

The technical means of communication of the battle group were inadequate. For example, there existed no radio communication between the dismounted staff officers of the panzer grenadier battalion and the headquarters of the battle group. Despite this, the various elements of the battle group managed to work well together.

Once it had finished its march on 27 November, the battle group had to be resupplied. Since the approach route to be taken by the supply companies was quite long, their arrival could hardly be expected until shortly before midnight.

## II. Specific situation

### 1. Task of Battle Group M

Towards 2300 hours on 27 November, the commander of the battle group received the order to clarify the situation in the vicinity of Hill 81.9, for communications had been lost with the strongpoint there. The battle group would be on standby so that, acting independently, it would be able to shatter any enemy attack near the hill and thereby maintain control of that position.

## 2. Preparatory measures by the battle group

It was not yet possible for the commander of the battle group to form an estimate of the situation. The course of action to be taken would greatly depend on whether Hill 81.9 would still be in the hands of the 97th Jäger Division by morning. It was to be expected that the enemy would want to capture the hill before he commenced his attack so that there would be no German artillery observation of his assembly of troops near Feldscheune. Our aerial reconnaissance had reported the presence of some enemy troops, but there were bound to be many more being assembled during the night. It could be concluded from the shift by the enemy of the bulk of his shock troops to the right half of the sector of the 97th Jäger Division that it was his intention to carry out his attacks on 28 November against the boundary between the 97th Jäger Division and the 335th Infantry Division.

The commander of the battle group therefore ordered that the resupply be completed as quickly as possible so that his formation would already be prepared that night for the inevitable encounter with the enemy attack. He also sent an officer reconnaissance patrol to establish contact with the command post of the battalion on the right wing of the jäger division, near the divisional boundary, to conduct reconnaissance of the terrain in that area, and to ascertain the status of our forces there.

At 0100 hours on 28 November, the commander of the battle group received the following radio message from the officer reconnaissance patrol (see figure 9): 'The enemy has been in possession of Hill 81.9 since 2300 hours. The positional battalion has been shattered. Its remaining elements have hedgehogged themselves 1.5 kilometres to the north-west of the hill. There are no communications with neighbouring formations. The terrain rises gradually towards the hill and offers no cover whatsoever.'

A quarter of an hour later, another radio message came in from the officer reconnaissance patrol: 'Tractors can be heard on Hill 81.9, and tanks on the other side of it. Our infantry forces are moving their combat outposts closer to the hill.'

### III. Assessment of the situation and plans for the conduct of battle

#### 1. Enemy situation

Our incoming reports showed that the enemy had created the preconditions that would ensure the safety of his troops as they assembled. He had even been able to exploit his success by advancing further during the night in the direction of Bolshaya Lepatikha.

The 97th Jäger Division would have been unable to gather forces quickly enough to plug the gap in the front, so the enemy, facing no resistance, could very well have advanced even further. However, it was unlikely that he would do so. Based on previous experience, the enemy would prefer to hold his tanks back and would refrain from hurling them forward into an attack at night. Nevertheless, the sound of motors on top of and on the other side of Hill 81.9 suggested that the enemy was preparing systematically for a powerful attack. In view of the schematic tactics employed by the Soviets, it was improbable that they would immediately pour additional forces through the gap, although it could not be entirely ruled out when planning our own conduct of operations.

We could nonetheless be reasonably certain that the enemy would bring strong forces, especially anti-tank guns, into position on the hill in order to afford his assembling troops better protection. It could also be expected that those troops would commence their attack at dawn.

#### 2. New task for Battle Group M

The loss of Hill 81.9 made the task to be carried out by Battle Group M considerably more difficult. Our artillery units would be unable to observe and fire on the enemy attack forces as they departed their assembly area, which would mean that the battle group would have to await the approach of those forces in open terrain. In the meantime, the bulk of the enemy rifle troops would be able to wait on the hill while heavy weapons moved into position and lay down fire on the entire combat zone of the battle group.

The commander of the battle group therefore took the decision not to wait but rather to retake the hill before the enemy moved forward. This would be achieved by regaining control of the old positions on either side of the hill and then seizing the hill itself from the left and right. The purpose of this assault was to get the battle group moving and to intercept the enemy attack before it could make any progress. It would be of great importance to try to separate the riflemen from the tanks and to bring their attack to a standstill in front of the hill. This could most easily be achieved if our artillery units could obtain a position from which they could observe the enemy and shower him with destructive fire. Because of this, it would also be important to find favourable observation posts for our artillery observers.

### 3. Possibilities for our conduct of battle

There were four options to choose from when it came to the seizure of the hill: (a) an attack at night led by the panzer battalion, (b) an attack at night led by the panzer grenadier battalion, (c) a panzer attack at daybreak, or (d) a panzer grenadier attack at daybreak.

#### (a) An attack at night led by the panzer battalion

An attack at night by the panzer battalion, supported by the panzer grenadier battalion, would have been nothing out of the ordinary for the well-trained and well-coordinated troops. However, attacks at night were always extremely costly if they were poorly prepared, conducted without a full picture of the enemy situation, or lacking in artillery support. They were also subject to failure if the night was not exploited in its entirety, for time would be needed to reach the objective, to go over to the defensive, and to withdraw the panzer troops before first light. But it was already partway through the night, and the panzer troops would have required resupply at the very moment the anticipated armoured enemy attack got going the next day. An attack at night by the panzer battalion therefore had to be ruled out.

#### (b) An attack at night led by the panzer grenadier battalion

Even the possibility of an attack at night by the panzer grenadier battalion had to be ruled out due to the shortage of time. Our attack would have lasted well into the morning, and this would have given the enemy the opportunity to see how the situation was unfolding and to change his own plan of attack. The weak panzer grenadier battalion would have become tied down and could very well have had to bear the full brunt of the new enemy attack on its own.

Because of this, the commander of the battle group decided that the panzer grenadier battalion ought not to conduct an attack that night. He would need it to maintain its mobility so that it could take the wind out of the sails of the eventual enemy attack. The panzer grenadier battalion therefore had to be kept at the ready.

(c) A panzer attack at daybreak

The panzer battalion was the most essential instrument for the conduct of defensive operations against the numerically superior enemy tanks. It primarily had to be kept on standby for this purpose. An attack with Hill 81.9 as a limited objective would have been too early a commitment for the panzer battalion. The result would probably have been a meeting engagement with the enemy tanks. Given the numerical inferiority of our panzer forces, it was far better to place them in favourable positions and to let the enemy armoured attack run into those positions.

(d) A panzer grenadier attack at daybreak

The only option that remained was a panzer grenadier attack at daybreak. This attack needed to be carried out as soon as possible so that we could take possession of the hill before the enemy began his own attack. Such a course of action was justifiable, for it would significantly enhance our ability to conduct defensive operations.

This attack would require correct use of the panzer grenadier battalion. It would need to remain outside the range of the enemy anti-tank weaponry on the hill whilst assembling its forces before dashing across the open terrain at dawn and capturing the hill in a single stroke. This meant the full exploitation of the mobility of our armoured personnel carriers if the action were to succeed. The troops of the panzer grenadier battalion would need to remain mounted on their vehicles as they covered the relatively long distance from their assembly areas to their objective.

## 4. Plan of attack

The decision taken by the commander of the battle group was that Hill 81.9 would be seized by the panzer grenadier battalion at the crack of dawn. The panzer battalion would initially be held back.

The plan of attack would need to be envisioned from the outset as both an offensive and defensive operation, and would thus have to be developed accordingly. The way in which the task was eventually fulfilled would depend greatly on the development of the situation. It had to be taken into account that our attack might run into that of the enemy. Should such a situation arise, the commander of the battle group was fully aware that it would be extremely difficult for his weak panzer grenadier battalion. The attack would have to be broken off, and the panzer grenadier battalion would need to make use of its mobility to disengage from the enemy. This could only succeed with the support of the panzer battalion, and it was for that reason that the panzer battalion was to be kept on standby. For the artillery, it was important that some of its observer units reach the hill alongside the spearhead of the panzer grenadier battalion. There was no time for preparatory bombardment by our artillery, as it was intended that the enemy be taken by surprise and that the panzer grenadier battalion achieve its success the moment dawn broke.

Until the commencement of the attack, the battle group had to maintain as much mobility as possible. If the enemy situation were to change before then, the battle group would need to be ready for action.

## 5. Order for the attack

At 0200 hours on 28 November, the commander of the battle group issued the following order to the commanders of the battalions:

1. Enemy forces of unknown strength took Hill 81.9 in a surprise attack during the night. It is known that the enemy is assembling large numbers of forces on the other side of the hill. An enemy attack from the vicinity of Feldscheune can be expected in the morning.

2. What remains of the positional infantry will cover the right flank on this side of and approximately one kilometre away from the hill. There exists no contact with the neighbouring formations.

3. The battle group is to retake the hill so as to create more favourable conditions for defensive operations against the anticipated enemy attack.

4. The panzer grenadier battalion is to prepare itself to carry out an attack on the hill. This attack will commence at dawn. The panzer battalion will initially remain in the hollow on the left wing and will be on standby in case it is needed at any time to support the attack of the panzer grenadier battalion. The panzer artillery battalion is to coordinate its efforts with the panzer grenadier battalion, while the panzer pioneer company will remain at my disposal. The flak battery shall carry out reconnaissance during the night, especially in the direction of Bolshaya Lepatikha, in order to find positions from which it can destroy any enemy tanks that might break through. Even while preparations are being made, all units are to ensure they are ready for immediate action if necessary.

5. Plan of attack: By fully exploiting our mobility, the attack is to be carried out in a single stroke and is to take the enemy by surprise. Once the objective has been reached, preparations will immediately be made there for the defensive battle. The panzer grenadier battalion is to hold on to the hill against any assault by enemy rifle troops, but it is to allow enemy tanks to roll past. The panzer battalion will be responsible for outflanking and destroying enemy tanks that break through.

6. I will be with the panzer battalion.

## IV. Course of the battle

### 1. Course of the battle for the panzer grenadier battalion

#### (a) Assessment of the situation and decision taken by the commander of the panzer grenadier battalion

The commander of the panzer grenadier battalion was given considerable freedom of action when it came to carrying out the task he had been assigned. He was unfamiliar with the terrain, and he also did not know the precise location of whatever was left of the positional infantry. It was therefore important that the nature of the situation and the terrain be clarified as quickly as possible. The conduct of the attack could not yet be planned in detail. Much would depend on the terrain to be encountered along the approach route and the degree to which the positional infantry could provide security.

For the second part of the task to be carried out, namely the defence against the anticipated enemy attack, it was vital that reconnaissance be conducted to find defensive positions. Should there be no time for the panzer grenadier battalion to dig itself in, the old positions would have to be used in addition to any the enemy had set up during the night. What also needed to be determined was where best the heavy weapons of the panzer grenadier battalion could be placed so that they could partake in the defensive battle.

The commander of the panzer grenadier battalion decided that he himself would find and establish contact with the commander of the positional infantry so that he could gain from him a better picture of the situation and thereby, hopefully, avoid any loss of time. Furthermore, he intended at the same time to move the panzer grenadier battalion forward from the supply area at Schäferei to assembly areas that lay closer to the objective.

After hastily being resupplied, the panzer grenadier battalion set of at 0300 hours and headed towards the hill. It was impossible in the pitch-black night for the troops to be entirely sure of their bearings.

(b)  Orders issued by the panzer grenadier battalion

While in the assembly area, the commander of the panzer grenadier battalion issued the following instructions verbally:

1.  The enemy is in possession of Hill 81.9. His strength is unknown.

2.  The positional infantry will cover the area two kilometres further forward on the right flank. The whereabouts of the neighbouring formations is not known.

3.  It is the task of the panzer grenadier battalion to annihilate the enemy forces on the hill at dawn and to retake the old positions there. The panzer grenadier battalion will immediately go over to the defensive after that, as it can be expected that the enemy will be launching a powerful attack.

4.  As far as possible, the troops will remain mounted on their vehicles whilst they execute the attack. The 1st Company will proceed on the right wing once it receives my order by radio, and the 2nd Company will follow in its wake. The troops of the pioneer platoon, also mounted on their vehicles, are to cover the deep right flank of the panzer grenadier battalion. On my order, the troops of the 1st and 2nd Companies will dismount and attack

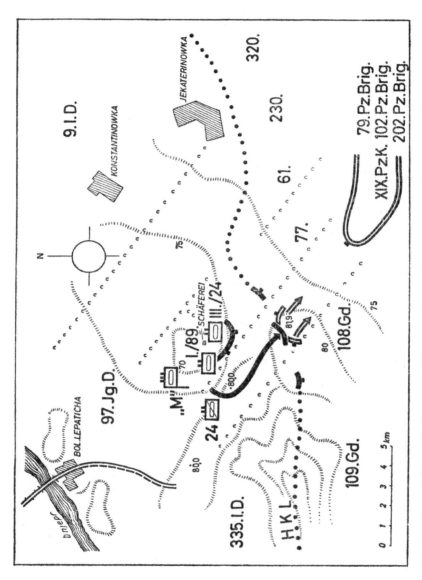

Figure 9: Second phase of the battle for Hill 81.9 – The panzer grenadier battalion (24th Panzer Reconnaissance Battalion) of Battle Group M retook Hill 81.9 at dawn on 28 November 1943. The Soviet 19th Tank Corps was at that moment preparing to launch an attack of its own.

the enemy on the hill. The 1st Company will strike from the right, while the 2nd Company will be echeloned behind and to the left. The enemy will thereby be hurled off the hill towards the left. Our heavy weaponry is only to be employed on my special order.

5. I shall make my way to the commander of the positional infantry.

## (c) The battle for Hill 81.9 (see figure 9)

After searching for some time, the commander of the panzer grenadier battalion found the commander of the positional infantry in a shelter on the right wing. This establishment of contact did not significantly change the planned course of action. It was determined that two companies would indeed be sufficient to seize the old positions, as it did not seem as if the enemy had significantly strengthened his hold on the hill. Furthermore, the terrain right up to the objective was easily navigable.

Approximately half an hour before daybreak, enemy artillery harassing fire began to rain down on the terrain leading to the hill. Light mist reduced visibility. The battalion commander thought it quite possible that the enemy attack would begin while it was still dark, so he ordered the commencement of our own attack shortly after the enemy artillery had opened fire. With its forces distributed in depth, the panzer grenadier battalion drove forward rapidly across the terrain that was being bombarded. It did not suffer any casualties. Daybreak enabled the silhouette of the hill to be seen from a distance of about 800 metres. The battalion commander had joined the 1st Company by then and gave the order for the troops to dismount. Light anti-tank rifles and machine guns started firing.

Both companies advanced rapidly and broke through the enemy positions on either side of the hill. The panzer grenadier battalion thereupon prepared itself for defensive action, with its heavy weaponry being brought into position and its unloaded armoured personnel carriers being sent to the rear. Only the vehicle of the battalion commander remained where it was, parked and camouflaged, so that radio communication could be maintained with the headquarters of the battle group.

The enemy began his attack approximately one hour after the break of dawn with preparatory artillery fire. His troops then left the assembly

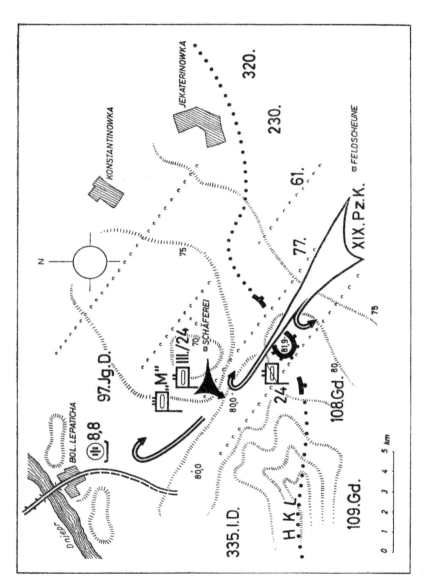

Figure 10: Third phase of the battle for Hill 81.9 – In response to the attack launched by the Soviet 19th Tank Corps, Battle Group M shattered the enemy rifle formations in front of Hill 81.9 and destroyed the enemy tanks after they had broken through.

area in the hollows near Feldscheune but were immediately subjected to our well-aimed artillery fire. The riflemen, some of them mounted on tanks, were forced to the ground. Despite this, roughly 50 enemy tanks continued with the attack, thrusting beyond the positions of the panzer grenadier battalion on a wide front. The enemy rifle troops, lying flat to avoid our defensive fire, failed to make further progress.

The enemy tanks charged in the direction of Bolshaya Lepatikha, but most of them were put out of action by the panzer battalion. Before long, the battlefield was littered with immobilised or burning enemy tanks (see figure 10).

## 2. Course of battle for the panzer battalion

After his formation had been resupplied approximately one hour before dawn, the commander of the panzer battalion made his way to a position on the left wing where he would be able to observe the progress of the advance of the panzer grenadier troops. The panzer companies remained on standby in the hollow to the west of Schäferei, ready to intervene at any moment.

When the enemy harassing fire began, the commander of the panzer battalion moved forward an assault-gun company so that it could provide the panzer grenadier battalion with fire support if need be. In view of the rapid advance of the panzer grenadier battalion, such fire support did not end up being necessary.

The panzer battalion therefore stayed back and, as soon as dawn broke, moved into ambush positions around the hollow near Schäferei. One company was given the task of covering the left flank against any enemy forces that appeared there. The other two companies moved into positions where they could await and destroy any enemy tanks that broke through the front of the panzer grenadier battalion.

Once the enemy had commenced his attack, it became clear that his tanks were headed straight towards the central part of the sector of the panzer battalion. The company on the left was accordingly brought back to the centre.

The concentrated fire of the panzer battalion brought about the destruction of most of the enemy tanks. Only a handful of KV-85 tanks managed to drive further, and they ran into the unloaded armoured personnel carriers of the panzer grenadier battalion. The armoured personnel carriers fell back to the north-west, and the last enemy tanks were finally eliminated by the heavy flak battery a short distance from Bolshaya Lepatikha.

### 3. Course of battle for the panzer artillery battalion

The commander of the panzer artillery battalion had made his way in his armoured scout car, together with the commander of the panzer grenadier battalion, to visit the commander of the positional infantry and thereby gain a better picture of the situation. He found out that there was not a single observer of the artillery of the 97th Jäger Division assigned to the area. He therefore assigned one of his own men the role of forward observer and placed at that man's disposal another armoured scout car.

The panzer artillery battalion stood between Schäferei and Hecke and, with its self-propelled guns, was ready to move and open fire at any moment. Once the German attack was underway, the commander of the panzer artillery battalion watched the movement of the panzer grenadier battalion from his vehicle. He was unable to order that the enemy artillery be targeted and fired on, for there existed no direct observation of that enemy. Poor visibility also meant that it was not possible to effectively support the panzer grenadier battalion as it advanced towards the hill. Nevertheless, the advance proceeded smoothly and had already achieved success by daybreak.

The forward observer dismounted at the same time as the panzer grenadier troops did so, and he then ascended the hill together with the 1st Company. Once on the hill, he positioned himself on the forwardmost line. The commander of the panzer artillery battalion ordered that, aside from some brief adjustment fire, the enemy attack would initially be awaited. Once that attack was underway, the enemy rifle formations in particular were to be targeted and destroyed. Having given this order, the battalion commander made his way back to the command post of the battle group. From there, as soon as it was reported that the enemy attacking forces had departed the hollow near Feldscheune, he instructed the panzer artillery battalion to fire at will. It was thanks to the sudden concentration of fire of the panzer artillery battalion that the riflemen were separated from the tanks and left behind.

## V. Lessons

### 1. General lessons

The battle for Hill 81.9 is a good example of the form of combat conducted by an armoured battle group within the framework of positional defence. The battle group fights independently in an area held by battle-weary positional infantry, which, due to a shortage of reserves, can only occupy individual strongpoints and cannot hold out against powerful enemy attacks.

Given that the situation was unclear, the orders issued by the battle group were rightly general in nature. Only on the spot could the correct decisions be taken.

Cooperation with the positional infantry was limited. Once contact had been made with it, the positional infantry helped to cover the assembly area and provided information on the local conditions. The XXIX Army Corps could do little to help Battle Group M, as it was unable to communicate with the positional infantry and was lacking in reserve forces. As is often the case in situations where the defensive fighting is long and hard, the only thing the army corps could do was to assign to the battle group the general task of holding on to or retaking a particular sector of the main line of resistance.

The battle group was consequently more or less on its own. Its commander had to clarify the situation and determine for himself the best way in which to conduct defensive operations. It was therefore right that he established contact with the endangered positional infantry battalion near the hill as quickly as possible before committing the battle group to a certain line of advance.

The battle for Hill 81.9 is also a good example of the way in which combat is carried out by small and mobile panzer forces in a relatively large area. The action on both sides was primarily conducted with tanks accompanied by infantry, while a subordinate role was played by the positional infantry.

Indeed, this example of combat remains valid even without the existence of positional infantry, especially given that future tactical warfare by mobile formations will require intermediary areas free of friendly troops. Rapid movements and sudden concentrations at focal points with the fewest possible forces will be the distinguishing features of such tactical warfare.

Finally, this battle demonstrates the effectiveness of combined arms. The various arms at the disposal of the battle group worked effectively with one another and were thereby able to reach their objective.

## 2. Characteristics of the Soviet conduct of battle

Demonstrated in this example is the schematic approach the enemy took in conducting his advance. He calmly carried out the one plan he had made beforehand, even though the situation had changed considerably. The plan probably foresaw the seizure of Hill 81.9 on the night of 27/28 November so as to create favourable preconditions for the security and execution of his attack. The assembly of the attack forces, which belonged mostly to the 19th Tank Corps, was to take place overnight. Those attack forces essentially constituted a long-range battle group whose task would be to advance rapidly on the morning of 28 November well beyond the hill and to take possession of the bridge in Bolshaya Lepatikha. There was no regard in this plan for the vulnerability of the flanks or the intervention of German reserves.

The failure to exploit the success that was the seizure of the hill was typical of the rigidity of the conduct of battle of the Soviet forces. The enemy ought to have immediately capitalised on his occupation of the hill by sending additional forces through the gap that had opened in the front. This would have made it easier for the tank corps to expand that gap the next day. It is likely that the Soviet rifle units had only been tasked with the capture of the hill, but this was insufficient if the enemy wanted to gain the initiative and exploit the weakness of the German defence.

The sudden recapture of the hill by German forces significantly endangered the departure of the tank corps from its assembly area. Nevertheless, the enemy stuck to his original plan of attack. Particularly vulnerable were his rifle troops, for they had no armoured personnel carriers at their disposal and were therefore exposed to German artillery fire. That exposure was deadly with the hill in German hands.

Although the enemy rifle troops could neither retake the hill nor penetrate the German position, the enemy tank attack carried on as foreseen in the plan. This attack may have been able to inflict casualties on the German infantry, but it blindly continued to roll forward and was subsequently eradicated by the panzer battalion.

The advancing Soviet tank brigades possessed poor fire discipline and were thus unable to conduct a proper firefight. None of the heavy weapons of the panzer grenadier battalion were destroyed, and not a single German tank was put out of action. Even the surprise appearance of the leading Soviet tanks amid the unloaded armoured personnel carriers, which were defenceless and parked in a hollow, led to no German losses. A few of our vehicles were rammed, but they were nonetheless able to escape.

The enemy was lacking in combat reconnaissance ahead of the bulk of his forces. Reconnaissance units ought to have fanned out from the point of penetration in order to obtain a good picture of the German defensive system. The enemy tank forces could have thereby avoided exposing their flanks to our well-positioned panzer battalion, and they might even have been able to manoeuvre skilfully enough to hit the flank of the panzer battalion instead.

On the whole, the attack carried out by the enemy demonstrated all the shortcomings characteristic of his tactics in 1943. He compensated for the lack of agility and skill of his junior leadership by adhering to the plan and driving forward senselessly. These weaknesses meant that the enemy was unable to utilise his numerically superior tank forces to full effect.

*3. German conduct of battle*

This example was chosen because it highlights the importance of the positional defence of key terrain for mobile forces. Holding on to key terrain is not an end in itself. Instead, it creates the precondition for the eventual annihilation of the enemy. What makes a particular piece of terrain 'key terrain' is that holding on to it is necessary if the annihilation of an attacking enemy is to be brought about. Furthermore, the capture of key terrain by the attacker gives him the opportunity to destroy the defender.

This example also makes clear the conceptual boundary of the counter-strike. The battle group carried out a counter-attack with a limited objective and, by holding on to that objective, was able to destroy the enemy attack that followed.

Also demonstrated in this example is that there is no fixed scheme for the employment of mobile forces in positional defence, as it depends entirely on the situation and the features of the terrain. What is important is that the battle group serving as a strike formation constantly carries out its own reconnaissance so that it can always be aware of the status of the positional infantry and can identify those locations where an attacking enemy is applying pressure. This enables the battle group to operate independently without having to await the slow or infrequent transmission of messages from the positional formations. In view of the foregoing, not only must the battle group receive reports from its ground reconnaissance units frequently; it must also monitor radio reports from tactical aerial reconnaissance at all times. If possible, direct signal communications should be maintained with the regimental command posts of the positional infantry, for the battle group needs to know precisely where friendly forces are deployed. Furthermore, attempts should be made to brief all commanders, right down to those in charge of companies, about the terrain in the anticipated operational area. In impassable terrain, it is advisable to take note of landmarks and of roughly parallel and perpendicular features so that it becomes a little easier for the troops to get their bearings. The use of standard battle maps showing locations of objectives facilitates cooperation, reconnaissance, and observation.

The commander of the battle group assessed the situation with accuracy. Launching an attack with the panzer grenadier battalion was a significant risk, but it was done with justification. If Hill 81.9 had not been retaken before the onset of the enemy attack, the bulk of the enemy forces could have advanced without being disturbed by our observed artillery fire. The enemy rifle troops, at least partly, could have followed the tanks into the depths of the battlefield, and the forces of the battle group probably would not have been strong enough to hurl them back. Moreover, the movements of the battle group would have had to take place within range of observed enemy artillery fire.

The decision to attack with the panzer grenadier battalion could be made with confidence thanks to the fact that it was a fully functioning and well-trained formation accustomed to mastering difficult situations through the exploitation of speed and mobility. Infantry without armoured personnel carriers probably would have been unable to reach their objective with the required rapidity. They would have been caught in the preparatory fire of enemy artillery while still in their assembly area. In contrast, the mechanised battalion could prepare itself far to the rear and evade enemy artillery fire by moving quickly. Its troops could then dismount just outside the range of the enemy anti-tank guns that had been positioned on the reverse slope of the hill and carry out the final part of the attack on foot. This type of attack, whereby troops dismount quickly and continue to move forward, places the highest demands on the capability and discipline of a formation.

Holding back the panzer battalion had also been the right decision on the part of the commander of the battle group. At dawn, the formation moved into a favourable position from which it could await and ambush the enemy tank attack. It would have been unable to provide much impetus to the assault carried out by the panzer grenadier battalion, as it would have only put itself within firing range of the enemy anti-tank guns on the hill and would have had to face the enemy tank attack in open terrain.

It was a mistake to leave the unloaded armoured personnel carriers so close to the front and in a position where they lay in the path of the anticipated line of attack of the enemy. They ought to have been withdrawn further and reassembled off to the side of that path.

Although it seemed as if the forces of the battle group had been split up, they worked together effectively at the decisive moment. While the panzer grenadier troops neutralised the enemy rifle troops, the panzer battalion saw to the destruction of the enemy tanks that had broken through. The panzer grenadier battalion had not been committed too early, and the panzer battalion not too late.

# Conclusions

## *I. Distinguishing positional defence from other forms of combat*

### *1. Counter-strike*

An attempt has already been made in Chapter 1 to distinguish between delaying action and positional defence. The purpose of describing the battle case studies showcased in Chapter 2—Nikopol, Moldavia, and Hill 81.9—was to make clear the distinction between positional defence and the counter-strike. While Chapter 3 will go into the tactics of the counter-strike, to be shown here in Chapter 2 is that there exists a considerable difference between positional defence and the counter-strike.

Awaiting the enemy is the one thing that these two forms of combat have in common. However, while positional defence places its emphasis on fire alone, the counter-strike unifies fire and movement. The objective of positional defence is only to hold on to a particular piece of territory. In order to achieve this objective, the attacker must be annihilated or at the very least brought to a standstill.[20]

Positional defence is defined in No. 146, TF/G, as 'holding on to territory against any enemy attack'. If the territory to be held is lost, positional defence can no longer be conducted. Retaking the lost territory demands that completely different combat principles be applied. Because of this, holding on to territory and retaking territory cannot quite be dealt with in the same breath. The terminology used to describe the principles of leadership for one form of combat must be distinct from that used for the principles of the other form.

The defensive position should indisputably be able to hold itself together well enough in order to prevent the enemy from achieving 'deep infiltration'. An occupied line with a 'trip-wire system' ought to suffice in this regard. Beyond that, the defensive position should be developed and occupied in such a way that will enable the enemy attack to be 'shattered or at least paralysed' and then 'destroyed in front of the position if possible'. Alternatively, the enemy should 'come to a halt or bleed to death' before the position (No. 155, TF/G).

---

20  No. 155, Para. 1, TF/G (1956).

This principle is no longer tenable. It leads to the establishment of closely connected positions that are either difficult to hold if forces are lacking or easy to punch through if the enemy possesses tactical atomic weapons. Positional defence must therefore be limited in scope from the outset and must be linked to the counter-thrust. Both forms of combat complement one another, just as delaying action is an independent part of defensive operations.

In this framework, the main task of the positional formations is to hold on to key terrain. Yet what makes a particular piece of terrain 'key terrain'? According to No. 155, Para. 2, TF/G, it is terrain whose occupation ensures the cohesion of positional defence. Such cohesion is intended to prevent an enemy breakthrough.

It is easy to imagine the existence of a defensive position consisting of a chain of pieces of key terrain, but such an idea is incorrect. A piece of terrain is only important for positional defence if its occupation creates the precondition for a subsequent counter-strike whose objective is the annihilation of the attacker. From the point of view of the enemy, that same key terrain is an objective of his attack. Should he manage to take it, he is likely to achieve a breakthrough.

A certain piece of terrain can enable the success of the counter-strike if its occupation: (a) restricts the movement of the enemy attack forces; (b) allows enemy movements, lines of advance, deployments, and reinforcements to be observed and reported; (c) allows observed fire to be laid down on those elements of the enemy forces, especially reserves and heavy weapons, that would not immediately be affected by the counter-strike; and (d) makes it difficult for the enemy to hit the flanks of the strike formations committed to the counter-strike.

It is not possible to go into greater detail here on the principles of positional defence or on how to conduct battle in a defensive position. Nonetheless, the point that can be made at this stage is that the counter-strike is on the one hand closely linked with positional defence and on the other a mobile form of combat whose principles are entirely different to those of positional defence. The principles underlying the conduct of the counter-strike will be investigated later, and it will also be shown that the counter-thrust need not automatically be carried out in every situation.

The counter-strike must be regarded as an independent form of combat within the framework of defensive operations that can be evaluated on its own terms. The principles for the leadership of strike formations must therefore be made clear.

## 2. Mobile defence and positional defence

According to US military doctrine, mobile defence is a form of combat distinct from positional defence.[21] The main difference is that forces are already committed in positional defence but are kept on standby in mobile defence. If most of the forces of a formation are occupying positions, then this is a case of positional defence.

It is doubtful whether this distinction could still be made in atomic warfare. The battle case studies of Nikopol and Moldavia demonstrate that even at that time, defensive success had been guaranteed by mobile action. The reason for this is that the forces committed to positional defence were often insufficient. It was possible back then for a positional system to be destroyed easily, and it has become more so today with the advent of atomic weaponry. Strongly occupied positions have become vulnerable.

Any defensive system has a mobile component, but the static and mobile components are too closely linked with one another in American doctrine: mobile elements serve as local reserves for positional formations in positional defence, with the conduct of battle focused only on holding

---

21  No. 182, FM 17–100, *Types of Defense*, defines these forms of combat:

   (a)  Mobile Defense. Mobile defense is the defense of an area or position in which manoeuver is used with the organization of fire and the utilization of terrain to destroy the enemy. The mobile defense makes maximum use of the mobile combat power of armour units; it is an active defense which employs offense and delaying action as well as defensive measures to maintain the defensive posture.

   (b)  Position Defense. In the position defense, the bulk of the defending force is disposed in selected tactical localities to maintain various positions and control the ground between them. The reserve is smaller than the striking force in the mobile defense and is used to add depth, to block, or to restore the position by counterattack.

a position, while positional elements are degraded to the status of mere cover forces in mobile defence.

The counter-strike and positional defence must be given equal emphasis. Only by clearly distinguishing between the two will it be possible to discuss the characteristics and principles of each.

# CHAPTER 3

# The counter-strike and the strike formations

## Introduction

In positional defence, reserves need to be created and kept separate from positional formations. These reserves are for the most part assigned tasks whose purpose is to hold on to strongpoints or to maintain a main line of resistance. Reserves are primarily intended to relieve or reinforce positional formations, to contain or eliminate penetrations of the front, or to execute counter-attacks.

The elimination of penetrations of the front has often been regarded as action carried out by positional formations. It has not been viewed as a measure arising from the conduct of field operations. Generally, little attention has previously been paid to the conduct of battle with reserve formations. No term was created for this, so speaking of a 'counter-attack' seemed to be adequate.

The battle case studies on Vesely and Facuti shall illustrate that the action carried out by a larger reserve formation in the hands of a senior commander cannot be described as a counter-attack. A completely new form of combat had been developed for the use of such formations on the Eastern Front, especially after the war there had become a defensive one. Armoured battle groups, referred to in front-line slang as 'fire brigades', were employed to conduct mobile warfare. While principles of leadership were developed for the use of these battle groups, they have thus far found little expression in field manuals or military literature.

The following couple of battle case studies will demonstrate that the counter-strike stands alongside and is therefore just as important as positional defence within the framework of defensive operations. Rather than being subordinate to positional defence, the counter-strike is an independent area of tactical leadership that requires special training if it is to be carried out properly.

A special term has not yet been created for the conduct of battle with reserve formations, so 'counter-strike' will be used here. It should be emphasised that the counter-strike is neither a counter-thrust nor a counter-attack.

Furthermore, since the formations in reserve are separate to those responsible for delaying action and those for positional defence, the term 'strike formations' will be used here when referring to them. In other words, for the three phases of defensive operations (delaying action, positional defence, and the counter-strike), there are special terms that refer to the formations involved (delaying formations, positional formations, and strike formations).

Each of the following two battle case studies was an individual engagement that occurred as part of a larger battle: one was during the battle for the Nikopol bridgehead, and the other during the fighting in Moldavia. Because of this, it is sometimes necessary to refer to the general situations around Nikopol and in Moldavia that have already been described in the second chapter.

The battle case studies on Vesely and Facuti are good examples of the employment of panzer formations whose strength and organisation correspond roughly to modern-day panzer brigades.

## Battle Case Study: Vesely

### I. General situation

#### 1. Situation in the combat zone of the IV Army Corps

The IV Army Corps held the eastern half of the Nikopol bridgehead, with all its divisions being committed to the front line there since the middle of November 1943.[22] Its sector was cut in two by the Belozerka Ravine. Between Vesely and the western side of the ravine stood the 79th Infantry Division in open terrain, while to the north of the ravine

---

22 See Chapter 2 for the description of the general situation around Nikopol.

was the 258th Infantry Division. Both infantry divisions were severely weakened and had no reserves worth mentioning at their disposal.

### 2. Situation of the 24th Panzer Division

The 24th Panzer Division was on standby in Znamenka on 19 November 1943. Commanded by Major-General Maximilian Reichsfreiherr von Edelsheim, the panzer division had created two battle groups that could be made ready to set off within 15 minutes:

1. Battle Group H (26th Panzer Grenadier Regiment, commanded by Lieutenant-Colonel Hans-Wilhelm von Heyden)
   a. Headquarters of Battle Group H
      • Flak squadron with 12 self-propelled 2cm flak guns (10th Squadron of the 26th Panzer Grenadier Regiment)
      • Howitzer squadron with four self-propelled 15cm heavy infantry howitzers (9th Squadron of the 24th Panzer Regiment)
      • Heavy squadron with three 7.5cm anti-tank guns and a pioneer platoon (11th Squadron of the 26th Panzer Grenadier Regiment)
   b. Medium panzer grenadier battalion of armoured personnel carriers (I Battalion of the 26th Panzer Grenadier Regiment)
      • Three panzer grenadier squadrons, each with 20 armoured personnel carriers
      • One heavy squadron
   c. Motorised panzer grenadier battalion (II Battalion of the 26th Panzer Grenadier Regiment)
      • Three motorised panzer grenadier squadrons
      • One heavy motorised squadron
   d. Heavy anti-tank battalion
      • Two companies, each with six of the 8.8cm Elefant anti-tank gun
   e. Panzer artillery battalion (II Battalion of the 89th Panzer Artillery Regiment)
      • Three batteries, each with six tractor-drawn 10.5cm light field howitzers

2. Battle Group M (24th Panzer Regiment, commanded by Lieutenant-Colonel Burkhart Mueller-Hillebrand)
   a. Headquarters of Battle Group M
      - Flame panzer squadron with 15 Flammpanzer III flame tanks (flame panzer squadron of the 24th Panzer Regiment)
      - Panzer pioneer company (3rd Company of the 40th Panzer Pioneer Battalion)
3. Panzer battalion (III Battalion of the 24th Panzer Regiment)
   - Two squadrons of 15 Panzer IV tanks armed with 7.5cm guns
   - Two squadrons of 15 StuG III assault guns armed with 7.5cm guns
4. Light panzer grenadier battalion (24th Panzer Reconnaissance Battalion)
   - Two panzer grenadier squadrons, each with 35 light armoured personnel carriers
   - One squadron of heavy armoured personnel carriers
5. Panzer artillery battalion (I Battalion of the 89th Panzer Artillery Regiment)
   - Two batteries of six 10.5cm Wespe self-propelled light field howitzers
   - One battery of six 15cm Hummel self-propelled heavy field howitzers

The remaining elements of the panzer division, especially the unarmoured panzer grenadier regiment, were also in Znamenka. However, rather than being organised into concentrated battle groups, they were at the immediate disposal of the divisional commander.

*3. Condition of the units*

The units were excellently trained, and their combat strength was at approximately 80 per cent. They were fully supplied and well-rested. Neither the XXXX Panzer Corps (Group Schörner) nor the IV Army Corps had any reserves at their disposal.

*4. Weather and terrain*

The light yet continuous rainfall in the days leading up to 21 November 1943 had made the ground muddy. Temperatures dropped close to freezing point at night. Sunrise was at 0730 hours and sunset at 1700 hours. The nature of the terrain has been described in the battle case study on Nikopol.

### 5. Situation in the air

Large formations of Il-2 ground-attack aircraft were at the disposal of the Soviet forces. This type of aircraft was slow but heavily armoured and could even withstand the fire of our 2cm flak guns. Nevertheless, the effect of this aircraft was limited; its guns were lacking in accuracy of fire, while its rockets or light bombs, though perhaps impacting morale, did little damage to the panzer forces.

Only small numbers of German aircraft were available, and most of them, in contrast to Soviet aircraft, were unable to take off in bad weather. The Luftwaffe could therefore offer little meaningful support.

## II. Specific situation on 20 November 1943

### 1. Enemy situation

At daybreak on 20 November 1943, the Soviets laid down a heavy barrage on the weakly occupied German positions on either side of the Belozerka Ravine. Large enemy rifle formations then moved forward at 0800 hours. They were supported by tanks and advanced to the north between Vesely, Nezamozhny, and Novaya Petrovka.[23] Multiple penetrations of the front were achieved against the desperate resistance of the numerically inferior German forces. Preparations were made by the reserves of the positional divisions for a local counter-thrust against the attack spearheads, but it was destroyed by the incessant enemy artillery fire before it had a chance to get going.

The enemy advanced almost unhindered after he had overcome our initial resistance. He soon approached our artillery units, which were still in position and firing.

---

23 See the military map of the terrain surrounding Nikopol in the appendix.

## 2. Task of Battle Group M

At 0830 hours, both battle groups of the 24th Panzer Division had assembled south of Znamenka, approximately one kilometre east of Ukraina, and were ready, depending on the development of the situation, to go into action.[24] The divisional commander made his way in his command tank to Battle Group M, whose forces were concentrated in the assembly area. Several armoured reconnaissance car sections provided reports on the development of the enemy situation and on the movements of troops belonging to our positional divisions. From the top of a large hill, the divisional commander was able to observe for himself the situation on the battlefield. At 0900 hours, he personally gave the commander of the battle group the following orders (see figure 11):

1. Strong enemy tank forces, roughly 100 T-34s, are to the west of the Belozerka Ravine and are advancing towards the artillery units of the positional divisions. In the Vesely-Nezamozhny area, our forces are sealing off the point at which the enemy penetrated the front, although he is carrying out multiple attacks of considerable strength there with his rifle and tank formations.

2. It is my intention to accompany Battle Group H and to confront the enemy forces that have broken through head-on, especially with the heavy anti-tank battalion, so as to prevent them from advancing further in the direction of Znamenka. Once the enemy spearheads have been brought to a halt, Battle Group M will strike the flank of the enemy to the north of the Vesely-Nezamozhny area. The objective is to cut off the enemy spearheads and to push them against the Belozerka Ravine so that the old main line of resistance can be restored in due course.

3. Battle Group M will roll forward at its own discretion, choosing a moment that will ensure the greatest chances of success in carrying out its assigned task.

4. I will remain with Battle Group H.

---

24  Znamenka or Bolshaya Znamenka. See the aforementioned military map.

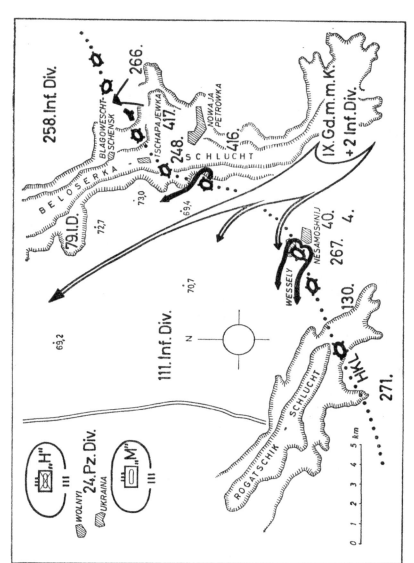

Figure 11: First phase of the battle for Vesely – The 4th Guards Mechanised Corps penetrated the front on the morning of 20 November 1943 and advanced parallel to the Belozerka Ravine. The 24th Panzer Division assembled its forces in readiness to strike this enemy.

### III. Course of the battle

*1. Assessment of the situation and orders issued by the commander of Battle Group M*

After issuing his orders, the divisional commander went to oversee the advance of Battle Group H. This battle group would have to rely on whatever forces it already had at its disposal.

The commander of Battle Group M ascended Hill 89.6, from where he had a good view of almost the entire battlefield. The battle group stood in extended order formation on gently sloping low ground and was ready to set off at any moment.

From his position atop the hill, the commander of the battle group was able to obtain a picture of the situation. Heavy artillery fire was being laid down on the German positions that extended all the way to the Rogachik Ravine. The noise of battle was to be heard from the Vesely-Nezamozhny area, and fighting was also taking place immediately to the north of that area, where some of our troops could be seen retreating. To the east of that same area, large numbers of enemy rifle troops advanced northwards over the hills that bordered the Belozerka Ravine. Swarms of enemy tanks were to be seen everywhere. The enemy spearheads, led by tanks and followed by riflemen, were approaching Hill 72.7, which meant that they had reached a point at almost the same latitude as Battle Group M. This advance was supported not only by a rolling barrage that moved slowly to the north but also by approximately 20 ground-attack aircraft that circled overhead.

Initially to the north-west of Battle Group M was Battle Group H, and the latter now drove forward to intercept the enemy spearheads. At its head were the heavy anti-tank battalion and the medium panzer grenadier battalion.

Battle Group H would have to face the numerically superior enemy forces in open terrain, and the commander of Battle Group M was concerned that Battle Group H would have a hard time of it. The panzer grenadier troops in particular would be subjected to the full might of the enemy artillery fire, and it was doubtful whether the heavy anti-tank battalion would be able to arrest the advance of the overwhelmingly large numbers of enemy tanks. Even so, this danger could not be allowed to discourage us from following through with the planned conduct of battle. Of great importance was that Battle Group M occupy the gently sloping Hill 76.9, which lay two kilometres to the north of the Vesely-Nezamozhny area. If the enemy managed to establish a firm hold on the hill, he would be in control of the intended route of advance of Battle Group M. What was worse, if the enemy had time to set up an anti-tank front there, as was his usual tactic when covering the flanks of an operational breakthrough, the effectiveness of the strike against the enemy flank by Battle Group M would be severely limited.

Nevertheless, it seemed practical not to commence the counter-thrust too early. The enemy needed to be given the opportunity to overextend his flank so that Battle Group M could slice through it more easily.

The commander of Battle Group M therefore decided that the advance would begin shortly before Hill 76.9 would fall into the hands of the enemy. Rolling forward any earlier would fail to produce the desired effect, as we wanted to ensure that the enemy would be intercepted by Battle Group H.

At 1000 hours, after almost an hour of waiting, the moment had come for Battle Group M to strike. This was because the noise of battle could be heard coming from the vicinity of Hill 72.7, and easily recognisable were the sounds of the fire of the 8.8cm guns of the heavy anti-tank battalion of Battle Group H. A reconnaissance patrol that was sent ahead reported that our infantry was engaged in heavy fighting immediately to the south-east of Hill 76.9, although the hill itself had not yet been taken by the enemy. The commander of Battle Group M therefore issued the following order by radio to the battalion commanders, all of whom had been briefed beforehand and were awaiting such an order: 'The panzer battalion will set off in the direction of Hill 76.9 and will attack the enemy tank forces to the west of the Belozerka Ravine. The panzer grenadier battalion is to follow the panzer battalion, while the panzer artillery battalion will monitor the progress of the advance.'

*2. Course of the first phase of the battle (see figure 12)*

In extended order formation, the panzer battalion lunged towards Hill 76.9 and, once there, opened fire on the enemy tanks that were advancing northwards. Approximately 20 T-34s were swiftly put out of action.

In this situation, the commander of Battle Group M received the following radio order from the 24th Panzer Division: 'Battle Group H is under attack from strong tank forces. To provide relief to Battle Group H, Battle Group M must speed up its advance towards the Belozerka Ravine.'

*3. Course of the second phase of the battle*

The commander of Battle Group M ordered the panzer battalion to advance to the old main line of resistance and, after that, to pivot to the north so that the rear of the enemy forces that had broken through could be struck from behind. As it moved forward, however, the panzer battalion was caught in the flanking fire of anti-tank guns from the area of the old Soviet main line of resistance. It became apparent that the enemy must have established a forward firing position there shortly before he had commenced his attack, and it was occupied by a number of light artillery battalions equipped with 7.62cm multipurpose guns.

The panzer artillery battalion of Battle Group M was immediately assigned the task of eliminating this anti-tank front, but it proved incapable of doing so, for the enemy position was solidly entrenched and skilfully camouflaged. The request made by Battle Group M for further artillery support could not be fulfilled by the 24th Panzer Division, as this support had already been given to Battle Group H and could not be taken away at that moment.

In the meantime, the forces of the German positional divisions that had fallen back to the north were reassembled and then committed to an attack whose objective was to reach the old main line of resistance near Vesely and Nezamozhny. All the artillery units at the disposal of the positional divisions would be needed for the support of this attack.

At 1500 hours, the commander of Battle Group M decided that the troops to the north of Vesely and Nezamozhny would have to withdraw from action, for his forces were simply not strong enough to destroy the enemy anti-tank fronts. He received the approval of the 24th Panzer

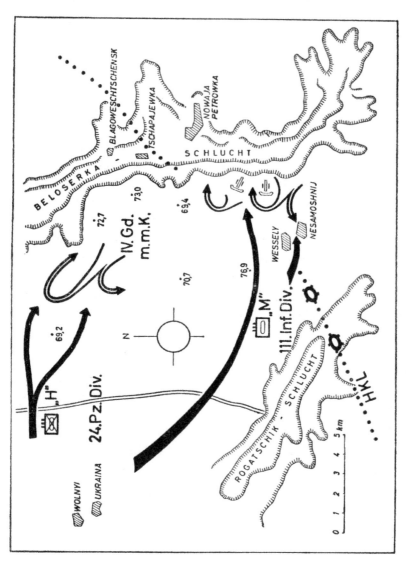

Figure 12: Second phase of the battle for Vesely – At noon on 20 November 1943, Battle Group H intercepted the forces of the 4th Guards Mechanised Corps that had broken through while Battle Group M launched a counter-strike deep into the flank of those forces.

Division in this regard and was ordered to assemble his forces to the west of Hill 76.9. Battle Group M would now maintain contact with the left wing of the infantry forces whose task it was to seal off the point of penetration near Vesely and Nezamozhny. If need be, the battle group would support and cover the left flank of the infantry advance. Another attack by the panzer battalion would be impossible, as it had expended almost all its ammunition in the preceding firefight and needed to be resupplied most urgently.

The supply companies had in fact been ordered by radio to move forward from Znamenka to Ukraina so that they could resupply the panzer battalion that night. Such a task could not be carried out in daylight due to the air superiority enjoyed by the enemy.

Meanwhile, the counter-attack launched by Battle Group H had brought the enemy spearheads to a halt and had even hurled them back to the area around Hill 73.0. We were able to observe the enemy as he withdrew his tanks that afternoon and sent them to the south, presumably with the intention of throwing them at Battle Group M. An armoured defensive line was therefore set up by Battle Group M so that our supply vehicles, directed by radio and light signals, could approach the front with some degree of safety.

### IV. Lessons

#### 1. Soviet conduct of battle

This example clearly demonstrates the way in which the enemy divided his attack forces between a shock group and a fixing group.[25] The shock group itself was divided into a long-range battle group (4th Guards Mechanised Corps) and a support group (41st Guards Rifle Corps).[26] Both artillery divisions were with that support group.

The fixing group conducted attacks with limited objectives to the east of the Belozerka Ravine in order to mislead the German military leadership as to the actual line of attack and to cause the German reserves

---

25  No. 106 FO RKKA 1936, which was revised in FO RA 1943.
26  No. 181 FO RKKA 1936, which was kept in FO RA 1943.

to be split up as a result of that. The presence of the ravine exacerbated this division of our reserves and could very well have led to disaster.

Typical of the Soviet conduct of battle was the mindless advance of the long-range battle group. It thrust to the north in accordance with a fixed plan that had been made beforehand, but the security of its western flank was inadequate due to a lack of strong combat reconnaissance there. This enabled the unhindered Battle Group M to strike the deep flank of the Soviet long-range battle group, which could have found itself completely cut off had it not been for the decisive action of the artillery of the support group.

Also typical of the Soviet conduct of battle was the employment of entire artillery regiments right at the front, whereby they would be brought into position on or even in front of the forward perimeter of the assembly area.[27] Such concentrations of artillery in the forwardmost positions were only possible thanks to the outstanding 7.62cm multipurpose gun, which could be easily towed, entrenched, and camouflaged. So that we would remain unaware of their presence, the batteries equipped with these guns did not take part in the preparatory fire prior to the enemy attack. Instead, their purpose was to provide cover for the assembly area and the safety of the advancing rifle troops against any armoured counter-attacks or counter-thrusts we might launch. Elements of these light support artillery units followed the rifle spearheads, and they succeeded in preventing Battle Group M from pushing as far as the Belozerka Ravine during the first phase of the counter-thrust.

Once the long-range battle group clashed with the heavy anti-tank units of Battle Group H, it became apparent that the Soviet operational leadership was lacking in agility. It ordered the long-range battle group to continue with its northward advance, yet it also withdrew the tank forces from that long-range battle group and committed them against Battle Group M. It failed to exploit the large gap that existed between the two German battle groups. An advance of the tank forces of the long-range battle group into that gap could have enveloped Battle Group M from the north, while any counter-attack by Battle Group

27  No. 190 FO RKKA 1936; No. 232 FO RA 1943.

H could have been kept at bay by the rifle forces of the long-range battle group.

Because those rifle forces were lacking in armoured personnel carriers, they had already suffered heavy casualties at the hands of German artillery fire by the time they attempted to renew their push against Battle Group H. They possessed no mobility whatsoever and had to dig in where they were. Without the tank forces by their side, they were no match for the panzer grenadier troops.

## 2. German conduct of battle

At the commencement of the Soviet attack, the German leadership decided at first to wait and see what would happen, and rightly so, for the operations of the 24th Panzer Division could only succeed once the main line of advance of the enemy had been clearly discerned. This battle case study shows how important it is to be familiar with the fundamental theoretical ideas of the tactics of the enemy. The Soviet conduct of battle stuck schematically to predetermined principles and regulations. The practice of dividing forces into a shock group and a fixing group recurred frequently, even in situations where local conditions did not permit a fixing group to be fully effective. This was undoubtedly the situation in the battle case study that has been presented. The enemy ought to have attacked on either side of the Belozerka Ravine at the outset so as to keep the German leadership in the dark for as long as possible as to where the main thrust would really take place.

Given the rapidly developing situation on the battlefield, the way in which the battle groups were to be employed for conducting a counter-thrust was to be left at the discretion of their commanders. Only they could assess developments on the spot and correctly determine when best to attack and in which direction to do so. It was therefore appropriate that the 24th Panzer Division issued orders that, on the one hand, specified the objective and stipulated the cooperation of the battle groups, but that, on the other hand, left it to the commanders of the battle groups to determine the details of the conduct of battle and even the timing of the commencement of the attack. If operations were to run smoothly, though, good telecommunications were essential, for only then could the panzer division remain constantly informed on the development of the situation and correct any course of action that might be going wrong.

Also essential was the conducting of thorough reconnaissance. The commanders of the battle groups needed to be aware at all times not only of the movements of the enemy but also of those of our positional forces so that the best decision could be made as to when the strike would begin. It cannot be overstated how important it was for the commander of a battle group to have a complete picture of the situation in his sector. He had to be able to accurately identify a particular point of culmination of the movements of the enemy if he wanted to precisely judge the moment at which his troops should move forward. If his timing was correct, he could allow an enemy breakthrough to proceed to such an extent that a thrust into its deep flank would have good chances of success.

That the thrust of Battle Group M failed to isolate or cut off the enemy long-range battle group can be attributed to the fact that it was carried out too deeply. It was because of the narrowness of the enemy breakthrough between the Vesely–Nezamozhny area and the Belozerka Ravine that the counter-thrust had been directed so far to the south. The intention was not only to relieve the left flank of the positional infantry of the 79th Infantry Division that was still holding out but also to completely cut off the long-range battle group that had broken through.

This deep thrust came within firing range of the powerful artillery, positioned far forward, of the Soviet support group. Battle Group M would have needed strong artillery units of its own to be able to overcome this enemy, but such units could not be made available by the 24th Panzer Division. The correct course of action would have been to place all the artillery units of the positional divisions, or at least all those that could have been employed effectively in this sector, under the command of Battle Group M at the outset of the counter-thrust so that fire could be concentrated at the point of main effort. Unfortunately, the artillery units of the infantry divisions were too poorly equipped at that time to be able to reposition their guns quickly, and, in any case, their forward observers could hardly move by day. On top of that, it would have been difficult for the artillery command of the panzer division to assume responsibility for the fire control of the artillery units of the infantry divisions, for their radio frequencies did not overlap. It is also worth bearing in mind that the positional infantry troops had to fight just as hard as the panzer arm, so it would have been a considerable challenge to convince them to hand over their artillery for even a short time.

As a result, the panzer forces earmarked for the counter-thrust mostly had to make do with whatever was available. Cooperation between the panzer arm and the positional infantry was limited. Both carried out reconnaissance and kept one another informed as to their intentions, but closer cooperation when it came to the conduct of operations could not be achieved due to the relative rapidity with which the actions of the panzer arm had to be executed. If the panzer forces had been placed under the command of the local positional forces, it could have easily led to the fragmentation of those panzer forces. Positional factors would have taken priority, while the need for counter-action could very well have been forgotten. Just as inadvisable would have been the subordination of the infantry to the panzer forces. It was the role of the infantry forces to bear the full brunt of the initial enemy attack, and they did indeed do so and were significantly weakened by the time the panzer units could intervene. The infantry then had to reorganise its units, bring forward the elements that had fallen back, and ensure the maintenance of the local defensive system.

The infantry would naturally need to exploit and gain any advantage possible from the action of the panzer forces, and this was indeed what happened when it carried out a decisive counter-thrust towards Vesely and Nezamozhny.

## Battle Case Study: Facuti

### I. General situation

*1. Situation in the combat zone of the LVII Panzer Corps at the beginning of May 1944*

At the beginning of May 1944, the LVII Panzer Corps conducted defensive operations in the vicinity of Targu Frumos in Moldavia.[28] It

---

28  Refer to the battle case study on Moldavia for more details on the general situation.

had a few weak German and Romanian infantry divisions at its disposal, but also under its command and committed to the focal point of the defensive efforts to the north and north-west of Targu Frumos was Panzer Grenadier Division Großdeutschland. Behind the right wing of the LVII Panzer Corps was the 24th Panzer Division, which had been placed in reserve by the Eighth Army and had recently left Jassy to reach its new position.

With its right boundary in the vicinity of Potieni and its left immediately to the west of Hill 192, Panzer Fusilier Regiment Großdeutschland, under the command of Colonel Horst Niemack, held a favourable defensive position that for the most part spanned a gently sloping range of hills. Further to the right were the lowlands of Belcesti, while to the left were further forces belonging to Panzer Grenadier Division Großdeutschland.

The overall task of the panzer fusilier regiment was to hold on to this position. In particular, the enemy had to be prevented from seizing the crossings over the chain of lakes near Facuti. Two battalions of the panzer fusilier regiment were committed to the forwardmost line in well-built field emplacements, while the third battalion remained on standby in the vicinity of Facuti. The village had been extensively prepared as a strongpoint to be firmly held, and it was there that the regimental command post was located.

Although the panzer fusilier regiment was at full strength in terms of men and materiel, a large percentage of those men were young replacements with no combat experience.

## 2. Situation and overall task of the 24th Panzer Division

Under the command of Major-General Maximilian Reichsfreiherr von Edelsheim, the 24th Panzer Division had been committed to heavy and costly defensive fighting in difficult terrain in the vicinity of Jassy prior to being shifted on 30 April to the area around Podu Iloaiei and Sarca, both of which lay on the road connecting Jassy and Targu Frumos. The troops were exhausted and could only be granted one day of rest, but they were at least fully supplied.

The 24th Panzer Division was to prepare itself for a counter-thrust against enemy forces that had broken through the front on the right wing of Panzer Grenadier Division Großdeutschland. Reconnaissance had to be conducted in order to find out which routes could best be exploited, and contact would need to be made with the positional forces. In fact, the panzer division was already on standby and had divided its forces into two battle groups:

1. Battle Group E (commanded by Lieutenant-Colonel Hans-Egon von Einem)
   a. two panzer grenadier battalions
   b. one panzer artillery battalion
2. Battle Group W (commanded by Colonel Siegfried Freiherr von Waldenburg)[29]
   a. Headquarters of Battle Group W (headquarters of the 26th Panzer Grenadier Regiment)
      • Headquarters squadron (11th Squadron of the 26th Panzer Grenadier Regiment) with a signal communication platoon, an anti-tank platoon equipped with three 7.5cm anti-tank guns, and a covering platoon
      • Infantry support gun squadron (9th Squadron of the 26th Panzer Grenadier Regiment) equipped with three 15cm infantry support guns mounted on Panzer 38(t) tanks
      • Flak squadron (10th Squadron of the 26th Panzer Grenadier Regiment) equipped with nine self-propelled 2cm flak guns
   b. Panzer battalion (III Battalion of the 24th Panzer Regiment)
      • two panzer squadrons (10th and 12th Squadrons of the 24th Panzer Regiment), each equipped with six to eight Panzer IV tanks with 7.5cm L/48 guns
      • one panzer squadron (9th Squadron of the 24th Panzer Regiment) with nine StuG III assault guns armed with 7.5cm L/48 guns
   c. Medium panzer grenadier battalion (I Battalion of the 26th Panzer Grenadier Regiment)

---

29 See image on page 98 for the organisation of Battle Group W.

- two panzer grenadier squadrons (1st and 2nd Squadrons of the 26th Panzer Grenadier Regiment) with a combined total of 18 medium armoured personnel carriers
- one heavy squadron (4th Squadron of the 26th Panzer Grenadier Regiment) comprising an anti-tank platoon equipped with three 7.5cm anti-tank guns, a gun platoon equipped with three 7.5cm L/24 guns mounted on armoured personnel carriers, an infantry support gun platoon equipped with two tractor-drawn 7.5cm guns, and a pioneer platoon equipped with armoured personnel carriers

d. Light panzer grenadier battalion (24th Panzer Reconnaissance Battalion)
- one panzer grenadier squadron equipped with 22 light armoured personnel carriers
- one panzer grenadier squadron equipped with trucks
- one heavy squadron comprising an anti-tank platoon equipped with three 7.5cm anti-tank guns, a gun platoon equipped with four 7.5cm L/24 guns mounted on armoured personnel carriers, a mortar platoon equipped with three 8.1cm mortars mounted on armoured personnel carriers, and a pioneer platoon equipped with armoured personnel carriers

e. Panzer artillery battalion (I Battalion of the 89th Panzer Artillery Regiment)
- one battery equipped with 15cm Hummel self-propelled heavy field howitzers
- one battery equipped with 15cm Brummbär assault howitzers

## 3. State of Battle Group W

### (a) Materiel

The battle group possessed only about 25 per cent of the number of vehicles it required. Its battalions were not that much stronger than ordinary squadrons. However, it had almost all the heavy weapons it needed. Each squadron of the panzer grenadier battalions had one medium mortar

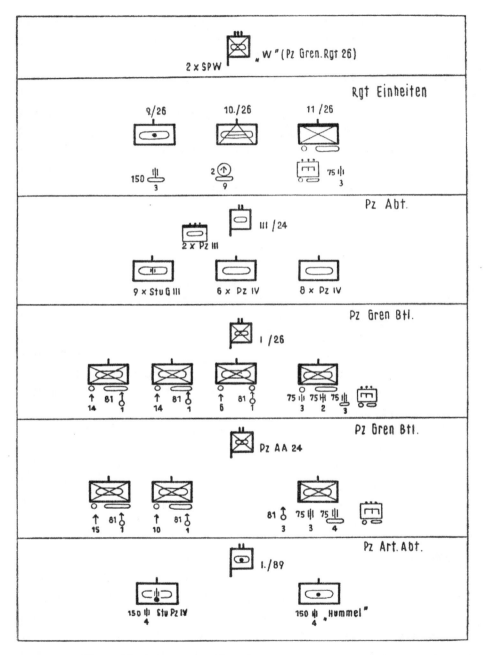

Figure 13: Organisation of Battle Group W on 2 May 1944.

and one or two heavy machine guns at its disposal. There were too few radio sets to go around, so while communications could be established between the battle group and the battalions, the same could only partly be done between the battalions and the squadrons.

(b) Personnel

The infantry forces of the panzer grenadier battalions were at about 60 per cent of required strength. About half of those infantry forces had lost their armoured personnel carriers and therefore had to be transported on trucks. This was a particular disadvantage.

Our units were led by young yet experienced officers. Many of the troops had fought for five years and had thus also gained considerable combat experience.

While the collapse of the front in Ukraine during the winter had greatly sapped the morale and fighting spirit of the troops, the successful defensive operations of the preceding month had elevated their mood and boosted their confidence. Only small numbers of replacements had arrived since the winter, but the combat experience, mobility, and quality of our military leadership enabled the troops to feel as if they could still demonstrate their superiority over the enemy.

(c) Supply

No supply troops were at the disposal of the battle group. It was the supply companies of the battalions under the command of the panzer division that were responsible for the supply of the battle group. These supply companies were stationed in Sarca, and they remained there throughout the course of the fighting, for the battle group was fully supplied.

*4. Weather and terrain*

There were several natural obstacles in the operational area of the panzer division that would limit the effectiveness with which tanks could be employed. Roughly from the area of Sarca, on the western side of the assembly area of the panzer division, three deep valleys fanned out to the west and north-west. Along the southern valley, which ran towards the west, was the main road that led to Targu Frumos. The middle valley ran through Facuti to the north-west and was filled with many lakes, yet there existed hardly any secure north–south crossings. The northern valley—the lowlands of Belcesti—contained the Cihadai Creek and was spanned by marshy terrain approximately two kilometres in width. This northern valley lay in front of our main line of resistance.

Between these three valleys were two ranges of hills, a distinguishing feature of which were their steep northern slopes. Those to the south of the chain of lakes dropped especially sharply, almost 100 metres on average, to the water below. In contrast, the southern slopes of these hills descended gradually. Only in some places were there valleys that cut through the ranges of hills from north to south.

We had only a few covering forces positioned along the high ground that bordered the lowlands of Belcesti. Any attempt by the enemy to approach these forces need not have been feared, as the lowlands would be difficult for the enemy to cross and easy for our troops to observe. Before the gently undulating ground near Hill 192, however, there lay an ideal area for the enemy to assemble his troops. The terrain climbed gradually from that area to where Panzer Fusilier Regiment Großdeutschland was situated and was thus favourable ground for the movement of enemy tanks.

Movement would be more difficult for the 24th Panzer Division, for there were no roads on the northern side of the main road leading to Targu Frumos. Multiple natural obstacles would have to be overcome, regardless of the direction taken, if the operational area held by the panzer fusilier regiment were to be reached.

Aside from some small woods here and there, it was predominantly uncultivated hilly terrain in the combat zone of the panzer division. Non-stop rain over the course of the last few days meant that it would be difficult even for our tracked vehicles to drive over the clay soil.

*5. Situation in the air*

It could be expected that the enemy would have a strong presence in the air at the outset of his attack. In particular, he possessed large numbers of the Il-2 ground-attack aircraft, which was heavily armoured and not easily destroyed, but which nonetheless had little impact on the panzer forces due to the inaccuracy of its rockets. Our tactical air units were available in limited numbers, and their use was dictated by the Eighth Army. None were assigned for cooperation with the 24th Panzer Division.

## II. Specific situation on 2 May 1944

### 1. Enemy situation

At dawn on 2 May 1944, the large-scale enemy attack commenced along the entire front to the north of Targu Frumos. The enemy succeeded in penetrating the front on the left wing of Panzer Grenadier Division Großdeutschland, and it became apparent that there were two main lines of attack in the area to the north and north-west of Targu Frumos. The first was a southward advance by strong tank forces from Bals along the road connecting Harlau and Targu Frumos, and the second was a simultaneous thrust by tanks and riflemen towards Hill 192. The preparatory fire of the enemy had been particularly heavy, the result of which was that he had already begun to make good progress.

### 2. Objective of the 24th Panzer Division

The 24th Panzer Division was under the command of the LVII Panzer Corps when the enemy attack began. It received the order that morning to carry out a counter-thrust whose objective was the annihilation of the enemy forces that had broken through the front in the sector of Panzer Fusilier Regiment Großdeutschland. After that, it was to work in conjunction with the positional troops so that the ground that had been lost could be retaken.

Because of the nature of the terrain, the panzer division was confronted with a difficult question in relation to how best to carry out its task. Should the bulk of its forces be committed on the northern side of the chain of lakes or on the southern?

If the bulk of the forces of the panzer division were to be utilized to the north of the line of lakes, it was to be feared that the numerically superior forces of the enemy would succeed in overrunning the positions of the panzer fusilier regiment and in seizing the crossings in Facuti. From there, the enemy would be able to advance to the south and south-west and crush the defensive position in Targu Frumos.

The panzer division could alternatively commit itself on the southern side of the chain of lakes, but it would then be questionable whether the old main line of resistance near Hill 192 could be restored. The enemy, given what we knew of his tactics, could be expected to immediately set up a strong anti-tank front near the hill equipped with numerous heavy anti-tank guns. He would thereby be able to exert his influence over the entire terrain that sloped downwards to the south as far as the chain of lakes. Furthermore, the commitment of forces to the south of the line of lakes would mean that the counter-strike would have to proceed via the narrow crossings at Facuti. This would severely limit the mobility with which the counter-strike could be carried out.

The decision reached by the panzer division was to place the point of main effort against the deep flank of the breakthrough area. Even if this might mean a temporary loss of the crossings, it was more important that the establishment of an anti-tank front on Hill 192 be prevented. At the same time, though, strong forces would need to be available to approach the chain of lakes from the south and deny any elements of the enemy forces that had already broken through there the possibility of advancing further in the direction of Targu Frumos.

*3. Course of action to be pursued by the 24th Panzer Division (see figure 14)*

The panzer division took the decision to initially split up its forces to begin with. The unarmoured Battle Group E, along with other forces directly subordinate to the panzer division like the pioneer battalion and the heavy artillery, would advance westwards along the main road and then wheel to the north to approach the lakes to the west of Facuti. In the meantime, the armoured Battle Group W was to proceed on the northern side of the chain of lakes from Sarca in the direction of Hill 192.

*4. Orders issued to Battle Group W*

Battle Group W received the following orders by telephone at approximately 0800 hours:

1. The enemy has penetrated the defensive position of Panzer Fusilier Regiment Großdeutschland at Hill 192 and is advancing with strong tank and rifle forces towards Facuti. It is obviously his intention to seize the crossings there.

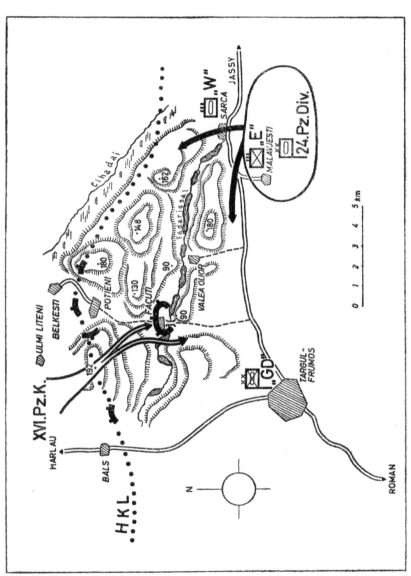

Figure 14: First phase of the battle for Facuti – When the Soviet 16th Tank Corps attacked and penetrated the front in the combat sector of Panzer Fusilier Regiment Großdeutschland, the 24th Panzer Division launched a counter-strike with Battle Groups E and W.

2. Our forces are involved in heavy defensive fighting in the main defensive area. Further details on the situation are unknown.

3. The 24th Panzer Division plans to annihilate the enemy forces that have broken through on either the northern side or the southern side of the chain of lakes. After that, it will restore the old main line of resistance at Hill 192.

4. The battle groups will set off immediately:

   a. Battle Group E will advance along the road in the direction of Targu Frumos until it reaches the turnoff for Facuti. From there, it will proceed to the north towards the lakes. Further orders will follow.

   b. Battle Group W will advance on the northern side of the chain of lakes from Sarca towards Hill 192 via Hill 148. It is to annihilate the enemy forces that have broken through and retake the ground that has been lost at Hill 192. Contact will then be made with friendly forces in the combat zone between Potieni and Facuti.

5. The command post of the panzer division will be placed one kilometre to the southwest of Valea Oilor.

## III. Course of the battle

*1. Assessment of the situation and decision taken by the commander of Battle Group W*

The commander of Battle Group W possessed no knowledge of the terrain through which his formation would advance nor of that in which the fighting was likely to take place. Although the 24th Panzer Division had conducted some reconnaissance as far as Hill 148 and had determined that the terrain until that point could be traversed by vehicles, there was no time available for any further reconnaissance.

The battle group stood in Sarca with the panzer battalion, the light panzer grenadier battalion, and elements of regimental units. Given that time was short, the commander of the battle group decided that his troops would forego further preparations and set off at once. Despite not having been able to gain a full picture of the situation, he was confident that this was the best course of action, as it was quite likely that the enemy would hurl forward strong tank forces in an attempt to expand the breakthrough area south-east of Potieni. The panzer battalion would therefore be the first formation to roll forward, and its objective would be to reach Hill 148 as quickly as possible. If the enemy had not pushed as far forward as expected by the time the panzer battalion reached the hill, it would nonetheless be a good location from which to reassess the situation and determine how best to utilise the battle group.

Shortly after receiving the orders of the panzer division, the battle group issued the following order to the battalions under its command:

1. The enemy has broken through the front at Hill 192 and is advancing southwards.

2. The 24th Panzer Division intends to destroy the enemy to the north or to the south of the chain of lakes. Battle Group E will therefore approach Facuti from the south, while Battle Group W will strike the enemy flank and re-establish the old main line of resistance at Hill 192.

3. In carrying out its task, Battle Group W will head northwards from Sarca and then approximately four kilometres along the main line of resistance beyond Hill 162 towards Hill 148. The panzer battalion will be at the head of the battle group, and it will be followed by the light panzer grenadier battalion, the flak squadron, the headquarters squadron, the medium panzer grenadier battalion, the infantry support gun squadron, and the panzer artillery battalion. This movement is to commence immediately.

4. The supply units shall remain in Sarca.

5. I will accompany the panzer battalion.

## 2. Course of the approach march

While the panzer battalion and the light panzer grenadier battalion managed to depart Sarca for the north without trouble, the remaining forces of Battle Group W were delayed due to the fact that Battle Group E had to make use of the main road that ran through the village as it set off for the west. Those remaining forces of Battle Group W were initially to the south of the road, and it was only gradually that they weaved their way through the movements of Battle Group E to the north.

The ground started to rise somewhat immediately to the north of the village. Progress was slow, even for our tanks. During the journey, the commander of Battle Group W ordered by radio that the leading panzer platoon accelerate its advance towards Hill 148 so as to scout the terrain ahead and provide cover for the German spearhead. Further forces were unable to be sent forward to conduct reconnaissance, for the wet ground

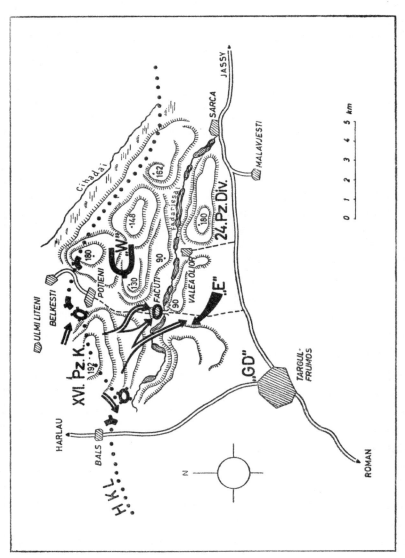

Figure 15: Second phase of the battle for Facuti – Battle Group E intercepted the enemy rifle troops to the south of Facuti while the positional formations sealed off the breakthrough area. Meanwhile, at 1100 hours on 2 May 1944, Battle Group W paused and concentrated its forces.

prevented rapid movement. In any case, the panzer battalion was the fastest formation and was already in front.

Even the light panzer grenadier battalion found it hard to maintain the pace set by the panzer battalion. There was no chance of it being able to make reconnaissance forces available. The terrain demanded that its troops advance in single file, and detours had to be made around a multitude of valleys with marshy ground.

The flak squadron, whenever possible, moved alongside the march column, occupying one stretch of high ground after another to secure the airspace above the battle group. Accompanying the commander of the battle group were the commanders of the infantry support gun squadron and of the panzer artillery battalion. There existed only radio communication with the medium panzer grenadier battalion, which followed in the wake of the rest of the battle group.

Only at 1100 hours did the battle group reach Hill 148. Many vehicles had fallen behind and had to be pulled out of the muddy low ground.

*3. Concentration of the forces of Battle Group W (see figure 15)*

Once the battle group had arrived at Hill 148, its commander received the following radio message from the panzer division: 'Enemy rifle forces have crossed the chain of lakes west of Facuti and are heading south. The positional infantry formations are still fighting at Facuti. Battle Group E is attacking from the south. Battle Group W must accelerate the execution of its task.'

The commander of Battle Group W was unable to see the battlefield from his position on Hill 148. Nevertheless, it was anticipated that enemy tanks would appear at any moment. He therefore took the following preparatory measures:

a)  As the fastest-moving means at the disposal of the battle group, a panzer platoon was given the task of advancing on Facuti via Hill 130 and finding whatever enemy forces remained there. The commander of the battle group would remain in direct radio contact with this panzer platoon.

b) All anti-tank platoons were to be brought into position on the reverse slope so as to provide cover for the battle group whilst also being ready to take the enemy by surprise if need be.

c) The flak squadron moved to the front of the combat zone of the battle group. From there, it could not only provide air cover but also counteract from a distance any enemy rifle forces that might materialise.

d) The infantry support gun squadron and the panzer artillery battalion were assigned the task of establishing themselves in positions from which their fire would cover Facuti as well as Hill 192.

e) The medium panzer grenadier battalion was brought forward as quickly as possible.

Thereafter, all the elements of the battle group were in position and ready for action, and it was not long before the panzer platoon that had been sent on ahead radioed a report from Hill 130: 'At Facuti, 30–40 enemy tanks of unknown type are in combat with the local defensive forces. The noise of battle is intense. Close combat. Southward movements, probably by enemy riflemen, can be observed to the south-west of the village. There is also considerable movement and noise near Hill 192. No German forces can be seen between Potieni and Facuti.'

*4. Annihilation of the enemy tank forces at Facuti (see figure 16)*

(a) Assessment of the situation

According to the assessment of the situation by the commander of the battle group, the enemy tank forces near Facuti were seeking to destroy the local defences so that they could seize the bridge or the crossing there. They seemed neither to have noticed the presence of the battle group nor, due to the nature of the terrain, to have any concern about their flank. The rifle troops of the long-range battle group that the enemy had hurled forward had already advanced beyond the chain of lakes, while the second wave was still in combat against our infantry near Hill 192. It would probably not be too difficult for Battle Group W to strike immediately to the north of and retake that hill. Even so, the possibility that the enemy tank forces would turn around at Facuti and drive into the flank of the battle group was cause for some concern. Given the tremendous explosiveness of the guns of the enemy tanks, it seemed as if we were dealing with a new, large-calibre, and long-range type. Only through the exploitation of the element of surprise could the destruction of the enemy tank forces be brought about.

If possible, the establishment of an anti-tank front by the enemy at Hill 192 had to be prevented; otherwise, the counter-thrust by the battle group would make little progress and would be unable to restore the old main line of resistance. Consequently, those forces of the battle group that were not initially needed for the attack towards Facuti were instead committed in the direction of Hill 192, although it was important that they not allow themselves to get tied down there. They were merely given the limited objective of preventing the enemy from positioning heavy weaponry on the hill and of working in conjunction with the positional infantry in sealing off the enemy breakthrough area. At the same time, measures were to be taken to provide cover for the assembly area for the attack towards the hill.

(b) Decision made and orders issued by the commander of Battle Group W
The commander of the battle group decided that it was an opportune moment to execute a surprise attack designed to bring about the destruction of the enemy tank forces near Facuti. For the time being, it was only necessary for the panzer battalion to go into action, while the light panzer grenadier battalion would be sufficient for the provision of protection. Due to the lack of clarity regarding the precise nature of the situation in and around Facuti, the panzer artillery battalion would be unable to do anything to help. To see to it that his decision was transformed into concrete measures, the commander of the battle group issued the following verbal order to the commanders of the battalions when he met with them:

1. The battle group shall destroy the enemy tank forces near Facuti.

2. To carry this out, the panzer battalion will immediately head to the south-west. In order to maintain the element of surprise, the slopes of Hill 130 are to be covered in a single bound and on a wide front.

3. The light panzer grenadier battalion will work in close cooperation with the panzer battalion. Once the enemy tank forces have been destroyed, the light panzer grenadier battalion will attack the enemy rifle troops near Facuti and relieve the German forces that are already fighting there.

4. The medium panzer grenadier battalion is to advance towards the high ground to the west of Potieni so that it can provide cover for the right flank of the battle group and establish contact with our forces currently in the village. It will then go over to the defensive so that it can prevent not only the expansion of the breakthrough area but also the positioning of heavy weaponry on Hill 192.

5. The panzer artillery battalion will support the efforts of the medium panzer grenadier battalion.

6. The infantry support gun squadron will remain at my disposal.

7. The flak squadron is to provide cover for the combat zone of the battle group from positions on Hill 130, ensuring that it can observe and fire on any enemy rifle units that attempt to move from Hill 192 towards Facuti.

8. I shall follow the panzer battalion.

## (c) Course of the battle (see figure 16)

All three squadrons of the panzer battalion commenced their advance towards Facuti and opened fire on the enemy tank forces as soon as they were within range. Our concentrated and highly accurate fire took the enemy by surprise. Although we still did not know what types of vehicles he had, 11 of them were destroyed within a few minutes. The enemy had no time to regroup and defend himself. Further tanks were rendered immobile by the panzer battalion, while the rest were blown up by the panzer grenadier troops in close combat.

In exploitation of the success of the panzer battalion, a squadron of the light panzer grenadier battalion lunged to the left and advanced to the bottom of the valley. It took the riflemen on the outskirts of Facuti by surprise and infiltrated the village from the east. The troops of the light panzer grenadier battalion remained mounted on their vehicles as they moved into the village and swiftly annihilated the enemy forces there. This action enabled the relief of the embattled and encircled headquarters of Panzer Fusilier Regiment Großdeutschland.

Meanwhile, the medium panzer grenadier battalion, also mounted, advanced directly to the range of hills that stretched from north to south

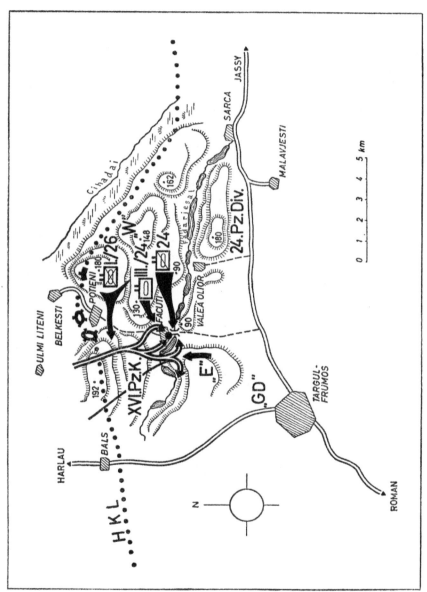

Figure 16: Third phase of the battle for Facuti – Battle Group W carried out a counter-strike and annihilated the Soviet 16th Tank Corps at noon on 2 May 1944.

at a point one kilometre to the south-west of Potieni. It established contact there with elements of the positional infantry and extended what had been its exposed left wing further to the west. The medium panzer grenadier troops then dismounted and forced back the weak enemy units. They could see the enemy on Hill 192, where the fighting had briefly subsided, but the German heavy infantry weapons and artillery now laid so much concentrated fire on him that he did not have a chance to do anything with his own heavy weaponry.

Once the situation in Facuti had been resolved, the battle group brought the panzer battalion into position behind the medium panzer grenadier battalion. The destruction of the enemy long-range battle group and the sealing off of Hill 192 meant that the conditions had been created for a counter-attack by the entire 24th Panzer Division in conjunction with Panzer Fusilier Regiment Großdeutschland, whose objective would be the recapture of the hill. It was carried out with tremendous success, but it will not be described here, as the battle case study on Facuti, as well as that on Vesely, is sufficient to illustrate the principles of the counter-strike.

### IV. Lessons

#### 1. Distinguishing features of the Soviet conduct of battle

The battle for Facuti is a typical example of the way in which major Soviet offensive operations had been conducted since 1943. The Soviet attack forces had been organised into a long-range battle group and a support group.

#### (a) Long-range battle group

The 16th Tank Corps was employed as the long-range battle group. Its main formation was a tank brigade equipped with the IS-1 tank, and it was the first time that this type of vehicle had appeared on the battlefield. Armed with a 12.2cm gun, this tank became the most formidable opponent of the German panzer arm. Also under the command of the tank corps were several motorised rifle brigades.

It was in accordance with the usual practice of Soviet tactics that this long-range battle group followed a detailed plan that had been made beforehand. The primary objective of this long-range battle group was clearly the seizure of Facuti, and it drove towards that objective without paying attention to its exposed flanks. The strong German resistance in Facuti gave rise to a certain helplessness on the Soviet side in view of subsequent events. Instead of withdrawing his tank forces and sending them towards the chain of lakes, the enemy doggedly persisted in his attempts to take the village. So poor was his reconnaissance that the counter-strike by Battle Group W took him completely by surprise.

Most of the rifle troops belonging to the long-range battle group were hurled forward beyond the chain of lakes. This corresponded to the Soviet practice of trying to establish bridgeheads wherever possible, even if with the smallest units.

(b) Communications between the long-range battle group and the rifle forces

What the battle for Facuti also demonstrates is how difficult it was on the Soviet side for communications to be maintained between the long-range battle group and the bulk of the attacking forces. The Soviet field service regulations from 1936 had the following to say on this matter in paragraph 181: 'It is recommended in most cases that the attack by the long-range tank groups be carried out in such a way that brings about the penetration of the enemy main line of resistance, that puts enemy defensive fire into a state of confusion, and that enables the exploitation of this confusion by the rifle troops and the combat vehicles accompanying them. A short distance should be maintained between the waves of the long-range battle group and those of the rifle troops so that the enemy is denied any time to reorganise his defensive fire.' In contrast to these field service regulations, and in imitation of German tactics, the Soviets were increasingly inclined as the war went on to form strong long-range battle groups and to assign them ambitious objectives. This approach was reflected in the organisation of tank forces into independent tank corps. In the battle for Facuti, it was clear that the Soviets had attempted to make the tank corps operate with complete independence and to send it as far ahead as possible from the main forces into the depths of German-held territory. Although the tank corps rapidly achieved a breakthrough, the enemy failed to exploit the confusion that had consequently been brought about on the German side. The bulk of his forces remained in the vicinity of Hill 192, albeit not long enough for large numbers of heavy weapons to be positioned there.

(c) Form of combat of the rifle forces

As was the case in the battle for Vesely, a characteristic of the Soviet advance in the battle for Facuti was that each success was to be secured through the establishment of a strong anti-tank front. Entire artillery formations equipped with 7.62cm multipurpose guns were moved far forward and camouflaged effectively. They presented a great danger to the panzer forces tasked with the conduct of the counter-thrust and were in the most general sense the backbone of the Soviet defensive system.

The enemy failed to establish such an anti-tank front on Hill 192 due to the fact that contact had been lost between the long-range battle group and the main forces. It was therefore possible for the German troops to separate and destroy the two groups.

In relation to this, a decisive disadvantage for the Soviet side was once more the lack of mechanised rifle forces. Such forces would have served as a connecting link and could have played an important role in conducting reconnaissance and covering the flanks. Furthermore, they might very well have been able to overcome the resistance of the German positional infantry at Hill 192.

## 2. Distinguishing features of the German conduct of battle

The battle for Facuti illustrates the conduct of combat with strike formations in mobile defence, and in particular the way in which the counter-strike is executed by large panzer formations. Even the decision made as to the initial use of Battle Group W greatly determined the degree to which the operation unfolded in our favour. It was by no means without risk that the battle group was committed to action even before there had been clarity on the enemy situation. However, the battle group could hardly have been sent in any other direction at that time, and only its immediate commitment could provide us with a chance of taking the enemy by surprise.

The enemy probably had not expected that our counter-measures would be carried out on the northern side of the chain of lakes. It did not seem to have occurred to him that his advance beyond those lakes would be exploited by the battle group in a 10-kilometre thrust, even though this was from our point of view the logical course of action. The main disadvantage for the battle group was its unfamiliarity with the terrain. It would have been ideal to brief the commanders of the formations of the battle group on the anticipated operational area prior to the commencement of the counter-strike, but it was fortunate that our inability to do so on this occasion did not diminish the extent of our success. With the arrival of the battle group on the battlefield, the enemy attack had already rolled so far forward, and its forces were so spread out, that it was possible to strike the enemy flank and to separate the long-range battle group from the rest of the forces.

It was the correct decision on the part of the commander of Battle Group W that the dangerous enemy tank forces be struck on the flank and taken by surprise. Situations that enable an enemy to be taken by complete surprise are rare, and there could have been no better way to combat the enemy forces equipped with their new and superior type of tank than to catch them unawares and hit them hard on the flank.

In the conduct of this particular counter-strike, there was nothing wrong with the division of the forces of the battle group. If the medium panzer grenadier battalion had been committed in the direction of Facuti, it would have been unable to do much more than what had been achieved by the light panzer grenadier battalion. The way in which it was used is an example of how combat missions with limited objectives are often capable of bringing about lasting success. Sealing off the breakthrough area at Hill 192 and preventing the establishment of an anti-tank front were preconditions for the subsequent rapid success of the attack against the hill, which was what finally ensured the resolution of the situation.

There was no radio contact whatsoever with the elements of Panzer Fusilier Regiment Großdeutschland that were encircled in Facuti. The battle group need not have conducted preliminary reconnaissance if such radio contact had existed, for a picture of the situation could have then been obtained from the panzer fusilier regiment. The arrival at Facuti of the battle group would have taken place earlier, and the many casualties suffered by the panzer fusilier regiment could have been avoided.

# Conclusions

## I. Distinguishing the counter-strike from other forms of combat

### 1. Attack

There is one important criterion that differentiates the counter-strike from the attack: while the attack is carried out against an enemy who is prepared to defend himself, the counter-strike is conducted against an enemy who is on the attack and not entirely prepared to defend himself.

The counter-attack is defined by NATO as follows, and does not correspond to the German usage of the term:

> Attack by a part or all of a defending force against an enemy attacking force, for such specific purposes as regarding ground lost or cutting off or destroying enemy advance units, and with the general objective of denying to the enemy the attainment of his purpose in attacking. In sustained defensive operations it is undertaken to restore the battle position and is directed at limited objectives.

> Attaque, par tout ou une partie d'une force défensive, d'une force ennemie assaillante, soit pour reprendre le terrain perdu, soit pour couper ou détruire les unités ennemies assaillantes avec pour objectif général d'interdire à l'ennemi la réalisation de ses intentions. En défense d'arrêt, elle est déclenchée pour rétablir la position de résistance principale et ne poursuit que des objectifs limités.

The attack generally requires careful rather than hasty preparation. In contrast, the counter-strike can only be planned in a short space of time, as it is entirely dependent on the conduct of the enemy.

The primary objective of the attack is territorial gain, while that of the counter-strike is unambiguously the destruction of the enemy. Territorial gain is only a secondary objective of the counter-strike. Because of this, the counter-strike cannot be spoken of as having a limited objective.

### 2. Counter-attack

The counter-attack is a special kind of attack. It is preceded by a hostile attack and carried out against an enemy who is prepared to defend himself. Its primary objective is to retake ground that has been lost. These two characteristics of the counter-attack—the prepared enemy and the recapture of territory—distinguish it significantly from the counter-strike.

Accordingly, the task assigned to a counter-attacking formation differs considerably from that given to strike formations. The order for a counter-attack is just like an order for an attack, but that for a counter-strike must do without a number of points due to their inability to be foreseen. The commander of the strike formations can only assign a general task to the effect that a certain enemy who has infiltrated a certain area must be annihilated, and it is up to the strike formations to determine the details of how best to achieve that.[30]

The modern regulations of foreign military organisations do not recognise the difference between the counter-strike and the counter-attack. In American military doctrine, the counter-attack is regarded as the task of the 'Striking Force' in 'Mobile Defense', although the details of its conduct are dictated by rules that are very similar to those of the counter-strike in the sense that it is presented in this book (see FM 1710, Nos 187 and 195). The way in which the counter-attack is understood here is in accordance with that presented in the TF/G.[31]

### 3. Counter-thrust

The counter-strike is the counter-thrust raised to the level of the conduct of field operations. Both hit the enemy while he is on the attack and not fully prepared to defend himself, both are initiated when the commander determines it is best to do so, and both aim at the annihilation of enemy forces that have broken through the front. However, the counter-thrust is so closely associated with combat by smaller units that it ought not to be used when describing the conduct of field operations.

---

30 Even Eike Middeldorf has not made a distinction between the counter-attack and the counter-strike; *Taktik im Rußlandfeldzug: Erfahrungen und Folgerungen* (Darmstadt: Mittler, 1956), 144.

31 For the history of the development of these American military regulations and the way in which the terms 'Striking Force' and 'Fixing Force' arose, see William Y. van Hook, 'Mobile Defense by Armor', *Armor: The Magazine of Mobile Warfare* (May–June 1957), 30ff, and Mitchel Goldenthal, 'Corps in the Mobile Defense', *Military Review* (September 1957), 14ff.

It is nevertheless worthy of mention that many of the principles of the counter-strike are the same as those of the counter-thrust. This is because the principles of combat are generally universal and are not independent of the conduct of operations. He who is unable to grasp a fundamental principle on a small scale will be unable to apply it on a larger scale and will therefore be incapable of mastering the art of leadership.

The similarity in the meaning of both terms has resulted in little attention being paid thus far to what distinguishes one from the other. The counter-thrust has often been regarded as synonymous with the counter-strike, but it is only the latter that correctly describes combat with large formations serving as strike formations.

## 4. Meeting engagement

The counter-strike greatly resembles the attack by a moving force in a meeting engagement.[32] Strike formations always maintain a developed formation at the very least, and this is the case even when they are on standby and not assembled for action in the sense described in No. 118, TF. In this respect, both the counter-strike and the attack by a moving force in a meeting engagement are the same.

The main difference is that, in the meeting engagement, the friendly force and the enemy one are both on the move. They are neither on the attack nor on the defensive. The opposing forces, incompletely deployed for battle, come across one another unexpectedly. Each side acts quickly and tries to be ready before the other. The attack must therefore be launched on a wide front while the troops are still moving (No. 116). Its point of main effort cannot be determined at the outset.

In contrast, the counter-strike takes place when one side is clearly on the attack and the other clearly on the defensive. Both sides are fully prepared for action. The attacker ought to be aware that a counter-strike might occur, so he can try to avoid being taken by surprise. This

---

32  No. 114, TF/G, only refers to the attack by a moving force in the context of a meeting engagement. This understanding is too narrow. It is possible for a systematic attack by a moving force to be carried out against an enemy who is prepared to defend himself.

counter-strike is conducted not on a wide front but rather against a point of main effort. This does not mean that the strike formations must be close to one another. Instead, if possible, they concentrate their efforts against the enemy at his weakest point from multiple directions.

### 5. Delaying action

Delaying action is related to the counter-strike. Delaying formations, just like strike formations, generally conduct battle independently and without being able to count on the support of neighbouring formations.[33] Both require that attention be paid to the nature of the terrain and the conduct of the enemy. Their commanders must be given the freedom to act and issue orders as they see fit.[34] Mobility and rapidity are characteristics of delaying action and of the counter-strike.

However, the objectives of the two are different. That of delaying action is to hinder the advance of the enemy, whereas that of the counter-strike is to completely destroy him.

Strike formations seek not to keep the enemy at a distance but rather to fight against him in such a way that will ensure his inability to retreat and that will thereby bring about his eventual elimination. Strike formations must therefore fully commit themselves to battle. They do not have the option of falling back to refocus their efforts elsewhere if the counter-strike is to succeed. This does not mean that a counter-strike cannot be broken off entirely and an attempt made to launch a new one at a different location, but such repeated shifts of focus are not as suited to the counter-strike as they are to delaying action. If a counter-strike is to be broken off, it must be because the commander of the strike formations deems it necessary for the avoidance of total failure.

## II. Principles of the counter-strike

### General principles

1. A counter-strike is launched against an enemy when he is moving forward with the bulk of his forces in an attack. In contrast, the

---

33  No. 214, TF/G.
34  No. 217, TF/G.

counter-attack is carried out against an enemy who is prepared to defend himself. The counter-strike cannot be planned in detail in advance, but it nonetheless meets the enemy when he is at his most vulnerable and often also on terrain with which he is unfamiliar.

2. The counter-strike aims for the annihilation of the attacking enemy, while the recapture of lost territory is only a secondary objective.

3. While the counter-strike might be able to shatter the enemy before he reaches the front perimeter of the friendly defensive position, it is usually the case that it only meets him once his numerically superior forces have already thrust well beyond that position.

4. The key to the success of the counter-strike is accuracy in its timing and placement. Such accuracy enables the interception of all the enemy attack forces and denies any of them the chance to defend themselves.

5. It is up to the forces that hold defensive positions to create the most favourable conditions possible for the execution of the counter-strike. They can do this by restricting the movement of the attack forces, by separating enemy tanks from enemy riflemen, and above all by preventing enemy heavy weaponry from being brought forward. Furthermore, the positional formations must make it difficult for the enemy to go over to the defensive.

6. Both sides could very easily grind themselves against one another from defensive positions, but it is much better to allow the enemy to move forward from his field emplacements into an area where he can be obliterated by friendly strike formations.

7. If possible, the strike formations should comprise all types of armoured and mobile forces. Panzer grenadier troops are the least susceptible to enemy artillery fire and can therefore be brought quickly to where they are needed. Panzer artillery troops are most effective not when they are caught up in the middle of an enemy attack but rather when they remain outside the enemy zone of fire.

8. A panzer grenadier brigade should always have its panzer battalion and panzer grenadier battalion ready as strike formations, while a panzer division should have at least a panzer brigade ready for the same purpose.

*Conduct of battle*

9. It is the responsibility of the panzer division to determine whether a counter-strike is to be carried out. The panzer division would ideally have at its disposal multiple strike formations in the form of battle groups or brigades. These strike formations would coordinate their efforts from several directions whilst maintaining considerable independence with regard to the details of the conduct of their task.

10. The correct decision as to the best time and place for the commencement of the counter-strike can only be made by the commander of the battle group or brigade tasked with its execution. He must familiarise himself with the nature of the terrain and keep track of the progress of the enemy attack.

11. In the counter-strike, it is best that the advancing enemy rifle troops are intercepted by friendly infantry or panzer grenadier troops while the advancing enemy tanks are simultaneously taken on by friendly panzer or anti-tank units. Enemy mechanised rifle troops that are on the attack must be compelled to dismount by the fire of friendly tanks.

12. It is particularly important that the counter-strike not enter the firing range of enemy anti-tank weaponry, which usually tends to be placed in the vicinity of the jump-off position for the enemy attack. If an enemy anti-tank front needs to be overpowered before the counter-strike can have any effect, then measures must be taken to organise and conduct a counter-attack against that anti-tank front.

13. Contact must be made with the embattled positional formations at the outset of the counter-strike. Such contact would ideally be by radio. This ensures that the commander of the strike formations can obtain a complete picture of the situation at any moment. He must above all be aware of the positions of friendly strongpoints,

the distribution of enemy forces, and the measures of friendly positional formations.

14. Throughout the conduct of the counter-strike, the ability for the positional and strike formations to cooperate with one another must be preserved. Coordination at even the lowest levels of command must be striven for.

# Conclusion

## Relationship between the three forms of combat in defensive operations

The principles of delaying action and those of the counter-strike have been presented in the preceding chapters, as has the difference between these two forms of combat and positional defence.[35]

Nevertheless, the relationship between all three forms of combat remains to be examined. Is each best thought of in isolation, or are they always inextricably linked, with one following immediately after the other?

1.  Delaying action can initially be regarded as something separate from the other two forms of combat in defensive operations. Large formations can be assigned the task of delaying the enemy without it being necessary for a defensive position to be set up further behind.

2.  In contrast, positional defence can only take place after, and therefore must be considered in relation to, delaying action. A defensive position requires that there always be at least one delaying line placed in front of it. This is the line of combat outposts. Should this line be overcome by the enemy, no further delaying action is possible, and it is at that moment that the positional defensive

---

35  See the following for the modern debate regarding the terminological classification of the various elements of defensive operations: H.-J. von Joeden, 'Elastische Verteidigung', *Truppenpraxis* (November 1958); *ibid.*, 'Raumverteidigung', *Truppenpraxis* (March 1959); W. Speisebrecher, 'Taktische Grundbegriffe der Abwehr', *Truppenpraxis* (January 1959); W. Kohler, 'Stellungnahme zum Beitrag "Taktische Grundbegriffe der Abwehr"', *Truppenpraxis* (May 1959).

fight begins. Even so, every effort must be made to bring about a return to ordinary mobile defensive operations as soon as possible. Due to the destructive impact that atomic weapons would now have on defensive positions, longstanding positional warfare can no longer be afforded. Both the attacker and the defender will have to do the utmost to maintain a state of mobile warfare.

Positional defence cannot even be considered as a temporary measure if there are no strike formations ready to carry out a counter-strike. Atomic weapons would rip apart positional elements and would thereby cause the positional defensive front to lose cohesion. Strike formations are therefore indispensable if defensive operations are to have any chance of success.

3. The counter-strike normally occurs after positional defence. However, it can also be conducted independently or take place immediately after delaying action.

The counter-strike can be conducted independently if there is no need to hold on to the terrain on which it takes place and if the reconnaissance of the strike formations is so comprehensive that the assistance of positional formations is not required. Such conditions exist in open terrain like deserts or steppes. In the foreseeable future, the perfection of various means of reconnaissance like radar, drones, infrared, and television may enable the battlefield to be monitored so thoroughly that the approach of the enemy can be spotted at an early stage.

The counter-strike can take place immediately after delaying action if there is no time or opportunity to set up a defensive position. It can be imagined that this type of counter-strike will be of increasing importance. By maintaining mobility, the impact of atomic weaponry can be reduced significantly. It is ordinarily positional formations that create the preconditions for the counter-strike, but if delaying formations can work in close cooperation with strike formations and create such preconditions in the last phase of delaying action, mobility would be maintained and there would be no need for positional formations. This way of conducting defensive operations would place such considerable demands on the ability of the formations and their commanders, and on the technical means of combat currently at their disposal, that it cannot yet be regarded as a generally applicable principle. Nevertheless, it is a capability to be aimed for. Its mastery will be a prerequisite for victory in atomic warfare.

## General principles of defensive operations

1. The defender awaits the attacker and compensates for inferiority in numbers with knowledge of the terrain and superiority in firepower.
2. In defensive operations, the attacker:
   a. is delayed upon his approach (through delaying action by delaying formations),
   b. is brought to a halt on key terrain (through positional defence by positional formations), and
   c. is annihilated or hurled back (through the counter-strike by strike formations).
3. If there are insufficient forces available to annihilate the attacker or bring him to a halt, then his advance can only be delayed.
4. Key terrain can only be held if there are enough strike formations on standby for the conduct of a counter-strike. In the meantime, delaying formations should always be pushed forward in front of such key terrain.
5. If strike formations cannot carry out reconnaissance or maintain awareness of the enemy situation on their own, they require that the enemy attack be delayed or that key terrain be held.
6. The commander entrusted with the conduct of defensive operations against an enemy attack in a particular combat sector should divide most of his forces roughly equally into delaying formations and positional formations. The rest should be kept ready as strike formations.
7. The delaying formations, positional formations, and strike formations in a combat sector should each be assigned their own commander. Depending on the nature of the terrain or the forces that are available, it might be advisable for multiple formations to be given the same task at the same time and for each to be allocated its own combat sector.

8.  Throughout the course of a defensive operation, formations originally allocated to but no longer needed for delaying action should be used to reinforce either the positional formations or the strike formations.

9.  Once the counter-strike has been carried out successfully, the strike formations must pursue the withdrawing enemy. If the strike formations are composed mainly of panzer troops, they ought not to be tied down to any position they may have reached during the counter-strike. Instead, it is better that they disengage and be put on standby.

# Appendix

# Maps

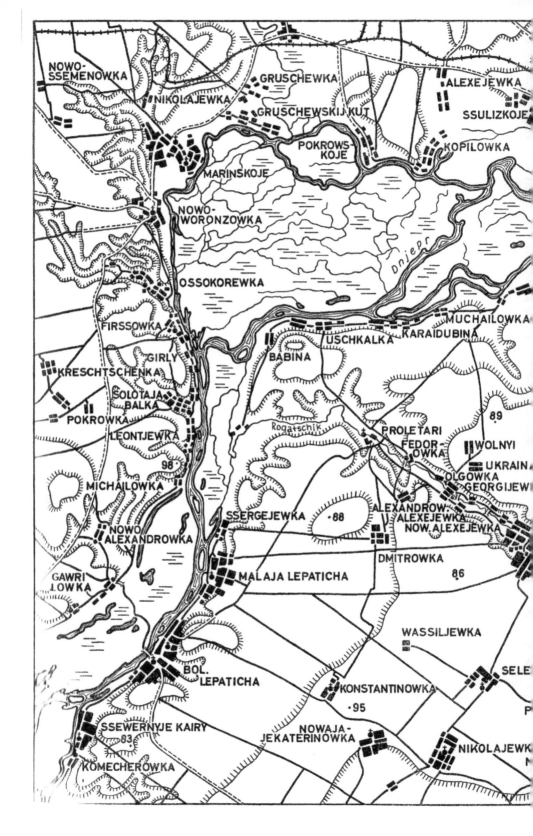

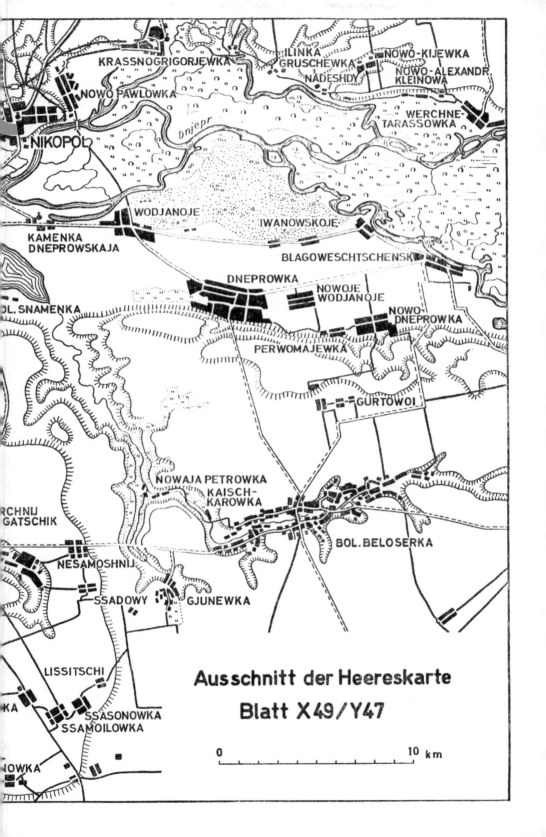

Ausschnitt der Heereskarte

Blatt X49/Y47

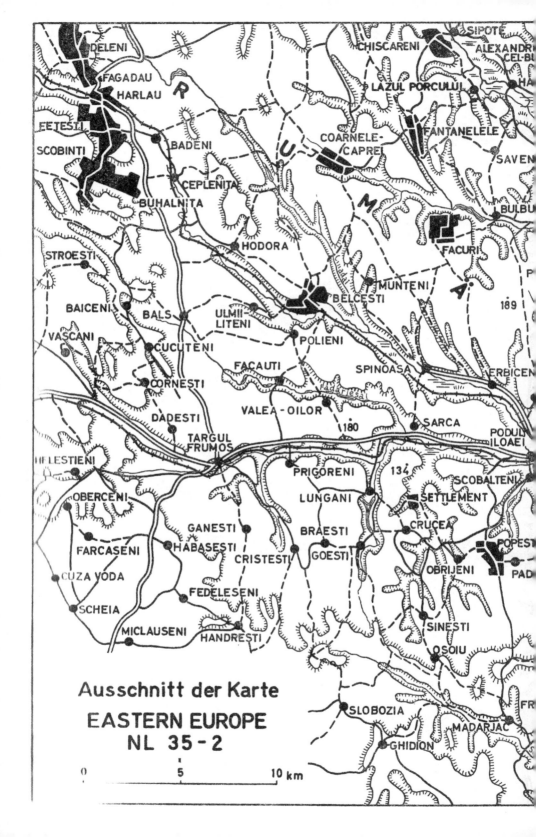

Ausschnitt der Karte

EASTERN EUROPE
NL 35 - 2

0       5       10 km

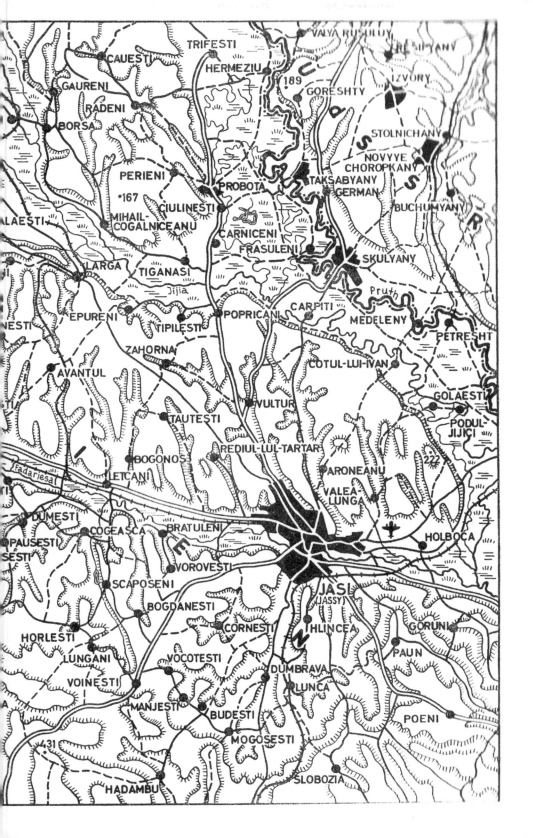

# Bibliography

## Documents

Combat report no. 3 of the 24th Panzer Division, Ia no. 420/44, from 12 May 1944.
Combat report no. 4 of the 24th Panzer Division, Ia no. 650/44, from 15 July 1944.
War diary of the 24th Panzer Division, November 1943 – May 1944.
War diary of the 26th Panzer Grenadier Regiment, May 1944.
War diary of the 24th Panzer Reconnaissance Battalion, November–December 1943.
Personal diaries of the author and of Gerd Becker-Wahl, November 1943 – May 1944.
Situation maps of the 24th Panzer Reconnaissance Battalion, 1 December 1943, and
of the 26th Panzer Grenadier Regiment, March–May 1944.

## Literature

### Military history

*Bronyetankoviye i mechanisirovanniye Voiska Sovyetskoy Armii* (Armoured and Mechanised
Troops of the Soviet Army). Moscow: 1958.
Fretter-Pico, Maximilian. *Mißbrauchte Infanterie: Deutsche Infanteriedivisionen im
osteuropäischen Großraum 1941–1944*. Frankfurt am Main: Verlag für Wehrwesen
Bernard & Graefe, 1957.
Friessner, Hans. *Verratene Schlachten: Die Tragödie der deutschen Wehrmacht in Rumänien
und Ungarn*. Hamburg: Holsten-Verlag, 1956.
Garthoff, Raymond L. *Soviet Military Doctrine*. Glencoe, IL: The Free Press, 1953.
*The German Campaign in Russia: Planning and Operations 1940–1942*. Department of
the Army Pamphlet 20–261a, 1955.
*German Defense Tactics against Russian Breakthroughs*. Department of the Army Pamphlet
20–233, 1951.
Guderian, Heinz. *Erinnerungen eines Soldaten*. Heidelberg: Vowinckel, 1951.
Kissel, Hans. *Gefechte in Rußland 1941–1944*. Frankfurt am Main: Mittler, 1956.
Shilin, Pavel Andreevi. *Die wichtigsten Operationen des Großen Vaterländischen Krieges
1941–1945*. East Berlin: Verlag des Ministeriums für Nationale Verteidigung, 1958.
Tippelskirch, Kurt von. *Geschichte des Zweiten Weltkriegs*. Bonn: Athenäum-Verlag,
1951.

## Tactical doctrine

Cushman, John. 'Pentomic Infantry Division in Combat'. *Military Review* (January 1958).

Department of the Army Field Manual FM 17–100, *The Armored Division and Combat Command*. Washington, May 1958.

*Felddienstordnung für die Rote Armee, Dezember 1943*. Berlin: General Staff of the German Army, Foreign Armies East, 1944 (FO RA 1943).

Goldenthal, Mitchel. 'Corps in the Mobile Defense'. *Military Review* (September 1957).

HDv 100/1, *Grundsätze der Truppenführung des Heeres*, reprint of October 1956 (TF/G).

HDv 100/2, *Führungsgrundsätze des Heeres im Atomkrieg* (TF/A).

Heeresdienstvorschrift (HDv) 300, *Truppenführung*, 17 October 1933, with Deckblatt D 36, 'Hinhaltender Widerstand', 1 May 1938 (TF).

Hook, William Y. van. 'Mobile Defense by Armor'. *Armor: The Magazine of Mobile Warfare* (May–June 1957).

Joeden, H.-J. von. 'Elastische Verteidigung'. *Truppenpraxis* (November 1958).

Joeden, H.-J. von. 'Raumverteidigung'. *Truppenpraxis* (March 1959).

Kohler, W. 'Stellungnahme zum Beitrag "Taktische Grundbegriffe der Abwehr"'. *Truppenpraxis* (May 1959).

Middeldorf, Eike. *Taktik im Rußlandfeldzug: Erfahrungen und Folgerungen*. Darmstadt: Mittler, 1956.

Middeldorf, Eike. *Handbuch der Taktik für Führer und Unterführer*. Frankfurt am Main: Mittler, 1957.

Smith, Albert H. 'The Battle Group in the Defense'. *Infantry: The Professional Journal for Infantrymen* (July–September 1958)

Speisebrecher, W. 'Taktische Grundbegriffe der Abwehr'. *Truppenpraxis* (January 1959).

*Taktische Zeichen von Wehrmacht und Bundeswehr (NATO) in Gegenüberstellung*. Heidelberg: Vowinckel, 1957.

*Vorläufige Felddienstordnung der Roten Arbeiter- und Bauernarmee 1936*. Berlin: Verlag 'Offene Worte', 1937 (FO RKKA 1936).

# Index